Law of Attraction Secrets

100 Powerful Affirmations for Instant Manifestations

3rd Edition

Nathan Powers

© **Copyright 2015 - Nathan Powers - All Rights Reserved.**

In no way is it legal to reproduce, duplicate, or transmit any part of this document in either electronic means or in printed format. Recording of this publication is strictly prohibited and any storage of this document is not allowed unless with written permission from the publisher. All rights reserved.

The information provided herein is stated to be truthful and consistent, in that any liability, in terms of inattention or otherwise, by any usage or abuse of any policies, processes, or directions contained within is the solitary and utter responsibility of the recipient reader. Under no circumstances will any legal responsibility or blame be held against the publisher for any reparation, damages, or monetary loss due to the information herein, either directly or indirectly.

Respective authors own all copyrights not held by the publisher.

Legal Notice:

This book is copyright protected. This is only for personal use. You cannot amend, distribute, sell, use, quote or paraphrase any part or the content within this book without the consent of the author or copyright owner. Legal action will be pursued if this is breached.

Disclaimer Notice:

Nathan Powers

Please note the information contained within this document is for educational and entertainment purposes only. Every attempt has been made to provide accurate, up to date and reliable complete information. No warranties of any kind are expressed or implied. Readers acknowledge that the author is not engaging in the rendering of legal, financial, medical or professional advice.

By reading this document, the reader agrees that under no circumstances are we responsible for any losses, direct or indirect, which are incurred as a result of the use of information contained within this document, including, but not limited to, — errors, omissions, or inaccuracies.

Table of Contents

Introduction 9
Chapter 1 11
The Law of Attraction and Affirmations 11
    Positive affirmations for divorcees 27
    For college students 36
    For new job 40
    For pregnant women 45
    For miscarriages 49
    For people getting married 53
Chapter 2 57
Some Important Affirmations In Brief 57
    Entrepreneur's Affirmations 57
    Rough Patch Affirmations 61
    Sex Affirmations 66
    Affirmations for Children 70
    Positive Affirmations for Elders 78
    Marriage Affirmations 82
    Mindfulness and Inner Self 87
    Inner Self 91
    When You Are Angry/Confused 95
    When You Want to Lose Weight 100
Chapter 3 107
Tips and Tricks 107

Chapter 4 113
Master the Art of Creating Powerful Affirmations 113
- Keep Your Affirmations Affirmative 115
- Keep Your Affirmations Within Your Vibrational Reach .. 116
- How To Get Instant Manifestations For All Your Affirmations 117
- Change/Master Your Thought Patterns 117
- Be Specific On What You Want 118
- Don't Give Rules To The Universe 118

Chapter 5 121
How Affirmations Actually Work 121

Chapter 6 127
Using the Law of Attraction to Attract a Partner 127
- Enjoy Being You –Right Now! 129
- Be Positive About What You Want from a Partner 130
- Keep the Faith 131
- Prepare for Love and Enjoy the Now 132

Chapter 7 135
Using the Law of Attraction to Attract Wealth 135
- Shift Your Focus Regarding Bills And Debts 137
- Realize How Much Abundance Is Already In Your Life .. 138
- Love Money 138

Chapter 8 141
Using the Law of Attraction for Professional Success 141

List What You Want From Your Job 143
Know That There Are Enough Jobs To Go Around 143
Chapter 9 145
Using the Law of Attraction for Weight Loss 145
The Gratitude Trick 146
Chapter 10 149
Using the Law of Attraction for Health and Wellness 149
Change Your Perspective On Illness 150
Conclusion 153
Publisher's Note 159
Your Free Instant Manifestation Gift! 161
Check out my other books 163
Sneak Preview of "The Lottery and Law of Attraction 165
Publisher's Bonus 169

Nathan Powers

Introduction

This book contains proven steps and strategies on how to create positive energy in your life using affirmations for instant manifestations based on the Law of Attraction. Basically, this is the belief that like attracts like. If your thoughts are positive, you attract positive things into your life, and if those thoughts are negative, then the energy you attract is also negative. These are all well-known phenomena and have been proven time and time again, but did you know how much they could affect your life? Many people underestimate their own ability to control the Law of Attraction, but that's what it's all about. It's about YOUR power and that's a mighty strong power to harness.

Do you believe in the power of affirmations in making things happen in your life? Do you know that you can have whatever you affirm manifested in your life instantly? This book contains 100 affirmations, which can be used in different situations to receive instant manifestations of anything you want. It also gives you strategies on how to create good affirmations in order to continue manifesting anything you require in your life.

The power of positive thinking is backed by scientific research – its not just some fairy thing conjured up by New Age types. This book will help you to use the Law of Attraction to bring the positive into your life and organize your thought processes so that you no longer attract bad things. It's a case of having the faith in yourself and the confidence to get where you want to be in life. Believe me, I never thought I would get there, but if I can do it, and believe me my life was extremely negative, then you can get there too which is why this book has been written. You can't keep a secret like this to yourself because everyone deserves positive experiences within their lifetime. This is my gift to you.

Sounds like an impossible dream? Well, it is not – you can learn all the skills you need to reprogram your subconscious so that all your thoughts are positive thoughts, which manifest into positive events in your life. Anyone can train themselves in the principles of the Law of Attraction – it's not easy, and it does require dedication on your part, but it is one of the most rewarding skill sets you will ever learn. What are you waiting for? Take the first steps on the path of positivity today and be surprised and amazed at how it works. One thing that is sure is that it will work.

Chapter 1

The Law of Attraction and Affirmations

Each of us are products of our own thoughts, whether we like it or not. Our current state is a product of our past and present thoughts. As part of the universe and as part of matter, which is all infinite energy, we attract the energies that we vibrate. This means that if we vibrate the right kind of energy, we can attract whatever we want instantly. The more you believe or want something to happen in a certain way that is different from your current state, the more you start manifesting that which you want. In this case, you will have infused vibrations that match what you want, resulting in you attracting what you want. Each of your thoughts is a vibration infusion that determines how your personal vibration will be; the more you expose yourself to a particular vibration, the greater its vibrational frequency will blend into your personal vibration. As the saying goes, like attracts like!

Although you can use different strategies to infuse vibrations that are different from your current state, affirmations stand out as strong tools that help you vibrate the right kind of energy that matches what you want. That means you attract that which you want in your life. Knowing which affirmations to say and how to transform your mindset to start vibrating the kind of energy you want to manifest is essential if you are to receive your manifestations instantly.

Remember, your affirmations should be focused on the ends (what you wish to manifest) rather than the means (how you intend to get the manifestations of what you want). Simply put, forget the means and focus on the ends throughout your affirmations. The more you focus on the means, the more your perceived difficulty in manifesting will be. On the flipside, thinking that your desires are being fulfilled changes your vibration to match what you wish to be manifested in your life. It also changes who you really are – you will build belief in yourself and become a much more confident person.

The law of attraction focuses on three simple steps; ask (affirm), believe, receive (be observant enough to notice the manifestations) and be thankful. Even as you say the affirmations outlined in this book, following these simple steps will keep the manifestations coming. Affirmations and the law of attraction go hand in hand. The more you affirm that something is going to happen in a certain manner, the more it will become a reality in your life. For instance, the more you affirm how much you are in love with someone, the more you will feel the love you have for them and the more you will feel that your lives revolve around each other. This will encourage you to have more experiences relating to the feelings you have for them.

Likewise, if your affirmations wish them to be happy, you will also have happy experiences yourself. In simple terms, the more your attention is focused towards certain life experiences that you wish to experience, the more those life experiences will manifest themselves. The more thought you give to your desires, the more apparent those desires will manifest in your day-to-day life. If you affirm whatever you want in your life, you start moving into a new vibrational zone; this is referred to as vibrational immersion in the Law of Attraction. Do you know that if you purposely focus your attention towards entering into a new vibrational zone, your life will start changing in a manner that reflects your close interaction with your intended vibrational zone?

Affirmations allow you to focus your attention towards the vibrational zones that you want manifested in your life, thereby allowing you to continuously transform your thoughts and perceptions to match with them. If your desired experiences manifest in your life, you can actually use vibrational locking to keep attracting that which has already manifested. Vibrational locking entails knowing your vibrational frequency at the time of manifestation of certain desires, in order to allow you to experience more manifestations in your life.

Affirmations are actually some of the best tools you can use to counter negative thoughts about things you don't want in your life; in this case, your affirmations should be positive. Don't just affirm that you don't want something to happen; say what you want to happen instead. This is the best way to start vibrating the right kind of energy that will attract the manifestations you want in your life. Here are 100 affirmations that will change your life by allowing you to manifest anything you want instantly. For ease of reference, they are organized into situations the in which you might want to say them in order to produce the manifestations you want so badly in your life.

If you are going through relationship problems:

- I like the way we are getting to know each other better.

- The love we have for each other will last forever.

- I look forward to our 30th anniversary when our kids are grown up.

- I look forward to the day I will walk down the aisle with you.

All of these are very positive statements. They reinforce the idea that you can affect the relationships that you have and you can also affect the direction in it, which they are going. You may be asking why then do relationships break up? The fact is that relationships usually break up because of negative circumstances. Letting too much negativity into your life will take it off course. People argue that the relationship ended because of someone else, but it takes two to tango and you need to make these affirmations together for it to be foolproof, and both are aware that there are repercussions for sliding back into negative ways.

If you are going through family problems:

- My family is inseparable.
- My family is the best family in the world.
- I love the way we love one another in the family.
- I love the way we all stand for one another in my family.

These all reinforce family values. If you let these rule your life, you begin to see problems within the family unit as being something that the whole family can pull together to fix. You believe in your family. You believe in hope and are able to use these positive attributes to make things work out for the better and to attract positive experiences.

If you are feeling worthless:

- I love every aspect of myself.

- I am a unique being of nature; without me, there would be an imbalance in nature.

- I know how valuable I am to myself and to those around me.

- I love myself unconditionally.

- I no longer criticize or judge myself for who I am now; I am free to love myself infinitely.

The problem with these is that you need to really say them and believe them. Don't doubt yourself. Look forward to getting to know the beauty of who you are. You really do have a lot more going for you when you think positive thoughts and all human relationships begin with self-love.

If you are looking for love from other people:

- I am always vibrating love; that's why people cannot help but love me.

- I always love and respect others just as I love and respect myself.

- I deserve love and always receive it in abundance.

- I am worthy of love.

Note No. 17. A lot of people don't get love because they don't consider themselves worthy. You have to believe that you are or this one will never work for you. It's vital to believe in it and to state it over and over until it becomes part of who you are.

If you want money or wealth:

- I attract money easily.

- Today is my day; money is coming to me in expected and unexpected ways.

- I deserve to be wealthy.

- I totally believe that I will attract money my way.

- Doors of opportunity fly open for my dreams to come to reality.

- I am becoming richer every day.

- My life is full of abundance.

This has actually worked for lottery wins! Those people who used the Law of Attraction to win money did so by envisioning having that money and believing in what that money would do to enrich their lives.

If you want a soul mate:

- My time has come; love is in the air, I can feel it and embrace it now.
- I am perfect and deserve the best just as I am now.
- I see love, I breath love, I move in love, I touch love, I perceive love, I smell love, love is me, I am love and love is me.
- I am now attracting the woman/man of my dreams.
- I love being with my soul mate.
- I am now divinely irresistible to the woman/man of my dreams.
- I am now attracting my perfect lover.
- I am now deeply connected to my perfect mate.
- My soul mate is now entering into my life.

- I am magnetic and irresistible to my perfect mate.

- My divine partner who I seek is also seeking me.

- I am destined to be with my dream life partner.

A soul mate is not someone that you meet by sheer fluke. If you use positive affirmations you actually get a better picture of what that soul mate is like and when you are looking for something that you can describe in a very positive manner, you are more likely to be able to find it through those positive thoughts. Don't ever let anyone tell you it's not possible. You need to believe that it is.

If you want a new job

- An amazing job opportunity will find me.

- Each one of my actions draws me closer to my dream job.

- I always impress employers by my skills and talents.

- I always attract perfect job opportunities my way; I am a job magnet!

- Promotions come my way every day.

- I am happy that I have found my dream job.

- So many job offers are always coming my way each and every day.

- Every time I receive a call, it is a new job opening.

- I will find my dream job today.

Although the last affirmation may seem a little unrealistic, it's not a bad one to wake up to every day. If it doesn't happen on that particular day, it doesn't mean it won't happen. It just means that tomorrow is another day and you need to repeat the mantra when you wake up tomorrow.

Affirm the type of friendships you want:

- I am always a loyal and straightforward friend who can be counted upon.

- I attract wonderful and truthful friends in my life.

- The universe gives me the type of friends I deserve.

- I find it quite easy to make new friends.

- I have a large network of wonderful friends.

- I love to socialize with others.

- I grow the number of friends I have every day.

Affirmations work particularly well to attract relationships. If you don't believe this, look at someone smile and see who smiles back. Positivity does that. If you put out positive vibes, you will always find yourself surrounded by people who want to be with you. It's part for the course, but if you keep up these affirmations, they will be there for you whenever you want to feel the warmth of friendship.

If you want to break a habit:

- I am gaining control of my habits.

- I know I am strong enough to stop any bad habit.

- I no longer find bad habits enjoyable.

- I develop new habits every day.

- It is easy to break bad habits.

- My self-control is immeasurable.

- I have strong willpower to overcome any habit.

- I am in charge of my habits today.

This one is all about faith in yourself. Habits are there because they are activities that you chose to incorporate into your life. Each time you perform them, you get this horrible negative feeling because you know what you are doing wrong. However, if you replace that habit with the habit of saying the affirmations, you get a really positive buzz from your own inner strength and that's much more lasting than the habit was and much more rewarding.

If you want to boost your self-esteem:

- I am a beautiful person.
- I am a valuable person.
- I am flowing with confidence.
- I have so many talents.
- I am very contented being myself.

Affirmations in this respect are all about learning to love yourself. Think about it logically, it you can't love you – who else can or why would they? You need to love your abilities; your possibilities; your potential; then you attract people because what you are able to offer them is something very complete.

If you want to affirm that you are attractive:

- My inner beauty becomes better with each passing day.

- I am extremely beautiful in all aspects of my life; my mind; my body and my spirit.

- I have beauty and brains.

- I feel more beautiful today than yesterday.

- I have the best smile in the world.

- I love every part of my body due to its incredible beauty

- I feel so good about my incredible hands, nails, hair, brains, skin and legs.

Attractive people attract others and perhaps you want to use your physical attributes to make people attracted to you. Make the most of them. You are a fortunate person and have lots of potential. By using these affirmations, you are reinstating every day that you believe in those attributes and will make them shine even more than they do now.

If you want to affirm how creative you are:

- I have an aura of creativity that follows me wherever I go.

- I become more creative with each passing day.

- I tap divine inspiration every moment of my life.

- I am always naturally creative.
- Creativity flows out of me.

Creativity is a wonderful thing. If you place a child in a room with a few bits and pieces to play with, that child will create a universe. Imagine what you can create by incorporating creativity into your life. If doesn't matter what form it takes. It could be anything from growing bonsai trees to creating paper cut outs. All that matters is that you look at what you create and see it as special. Don't always expect others to see things the way you want them to. You will create something that is unique to you and that is what matters. Try to remain as affirmative as possible and write down positive affirmations that will allow your natural talents to flow through you.

Affirmations relating to your health:

- I always admire my body.
- I am healthy and will always be healthy.
- I have an excellent vision, hearing and heartbeat.
- My body has an excellence metabolism.
- My spine gets better each day.

Health affirmations have to take into account your current state of health, but also have to see that current state of health as positive. How can you do that when you are crippled with arthritis? You can tell yourself that you are a very fortunate person and that you are able to adapt to it. People who are dying from cancer may be filled with positivity because they want to fill every moment of their lives with something worthwhile. Thus, no matter what ailments you have, surround yourself with positive vibes and your life becomes much more worthwhile.

Affirmations relating to time management:

- My time management skills today are better than yesterday.

- I get better at managing my time with each passing day.

- I have a clear plan of what I do every minute.

- I make every moment I spend valuable in my life.

- All my life unfolds at an excellent speed.

- My ability to manage my time well saves me so much time.

- I can account for every minute I spend doing things in my life.

- I do the right thing at the right time at the right place.

These are great affirmations for people who are not that good at keeping their timing correctly. Place them on the door of the refrigerator. Congratulate yourself every time you achieve a goal on time and make it become part of who you are. It can be. It is also a good idea to gift yourself something expensive. That will remind you about how you actually changed an old habit. Don't kick yourself for the occasional slip up, but go on thinking in a positive way, so that punctuality becomes part of who you are.

Affirmations relating to connecting with the spiritual realm:

- The universe is always trying to connect with me.
- I am well connected with my universe.
- I always get a response from the spiritual realm.
- The divine is there to guide me in everything I do.
- I am fully connected to my creator, the giver of infinite intelligence.

These affirmations can be backed up with a visit to a place of beauty because in this place of beauty, when you let all of the countryside caress your soul, you begin to see how small you are as a human. That's not a bad thing. That's a very good thing because it teaches you humility and it is by learning this that you come close to your creator and are able to develop an inner feeling of spirituality.

Affirmations relating to manifesting the law of attraction in your life:

- I accept every moment as my creation.

- I have the power to create my life the way I want it.

- I create miracles every moment.

- I vibrate the right kind of energy to manifest everything I want now.

- My present self is a perfect picture of everything I visualized.

Remember to be assertive with your affirmations. It should be short and to the point. Don't get too fancy with it. Keep it meaningful and to the point.

Positive affirmations for divorcees

Divorce is a harrowing experience for anyone. Not only does it affect the person going through the divorce but also their near and dear ones. Let us look at some positive affirmations that will help people going through divorces remain positive.

(For men)

<u>I will get through this</u>

It is important for the men to remain as positive through a divorce as possible. It is mostly thought that the woman will need all the help and support but in fact, it is the men who need it most. It is important that the man believe in his capabilities of moving forward from the bad experience. Reciting this chant regularly will help the man in a big way.

<u>I will be there for my children</u>

When two people get divorced, the children suffer the most. So it is important that, you, as the father of the children, remain supportive and be there for your children. Try to be their friend in this situation and make sure that they are comfortable. It doesn't matter how old they are, they will continue to be your children and it is important that you put their needs before yours.

<u>I will support my family</u>

As was mentioned earlier, apart from the two people getting divorced, the immediate families also get affected by it. So in times such as these, it is important that you support them as well.

Whether it is your mother or your father, be there for them and support them through the tough time. Recite this chant every morning and see to it that they are happy. Don't assume that they will cope with it by themselves without your support. They will need just as much emotional support as you and the two of you can support each other.

I will find new love

Divorce is not the end of the world. Don't think your love life is fully done with. Look to the future and tell yourself that you will find new love. Don't build a high wall around you and not allow anyone to come in. you must remain positive and encourage a little love flowing into your life. Although it might not immediately be possible for you, it is important that you not extend it too long. Tell yourself every day that new love will come into your life and that you will be happy again.

I will take care of myself physically

Many men start to ignore their physical well-being and end up turning into couch potatoes. They will also start growing a beard and drink every day. All this is extremely bad and not healthy for any man. If you start letting yourself go physically, then not only will others avoid you but you yourself will start feeling repulsed. So try to not let go of yourself and maintain your physical appearance and hygiene. Saying this affirmation on a daily basis will ensure that you actually do all of it without fail.

I will take care of myself mentally, emotionally

Don't let go of your emotional self. It is important that you get in touch with your emotional side and sort out any issues. Penting up your emotions is a very bad idea. It will start eating away inside your head. Try to vent out your emotions every now and then. The same goes towards mental upheavals. Let go of it if you wish to remain positive and have a healthy life. You will see a marked difference in your life and start feeling better about the situation in no time.

I will respect my separated spouse

When you go through a divorce, feelings of hate are sure to arise. As much as you think it is for the best that it has happened, you will feel like hating your partner for the rest of your life. But it is important that you not allow this hate to go on for life and start respecting your separated spouse and their decisions. Maintaining a civil relationship is always best as compared to fighting with them or ignoring them. If it is possible then cut all ties with them but if that is not possible and the two of you have children together then it is best to give and seek respect.

I will remain thankful to god

Many people start hating god when they go through a divorce and think that god has decided to put them in that situation. But this will only worsen the person's mental health. Try not to pin the blame on god. You will feel much better if you visit a religious place. The aura present at the place will help remove negativity. So thank god every day and recite this chant in your mind as often as possible. Remember that everything happens for a reason and if you went through a divorce, then it was meant to be.

I will improve myself

Many people don't understand that there might be something about them that drove their partner away. They keep thinking that the fault entirely lay with their partner only and they are not to be blamed. But this is not right. It is best that you conduct some self-introspection to see what is wrong with your personality and then work towards fixing it. Promise yourself that you will improve your personality and try to be a better person. With time, you will yourself start to realize where you were going wrong and how you can fix it for yourself. You will be a better spouse to your next partner and chances of that relationship thriving will be quite high.

I will be forgiving

After a divorce, it is common for the person to turn quite bitter. But it is important that you not turn that way and learn to forgive and forget. You will develop a sort of resistance and be in a position to forgive others that rub you're the wrong way. You will not feel the need to lose your cool and will remain positive all though out.

These form the different positive affirmations that men need to recite if they wish to get through a divorce smoothly.

(For women)

I will remain positive

A divorce can have a very big mental impact on a woman. All sorts of negative thoughts will start to crop up including feeling rejected and dejected. But it is important that the woman remain as positive as possible. Don't think negatively about anything at all and remain as positive as possible, especially in your outlook towards life. This phase will surely pass and you will have your life back. Chant this affirmation on a daily basis and you can also write it down on your cell phone and read it out loud every once in a while to remain motivated and happy.

I am blessed to have my children

For women, their biggest support system during divorce will be her children. You have to count your blessings and be thankful for having your children in your life. Try to remain as positive for their sake and support them. You will find it extremely easy to sail through your divorce if you have your children's support and so, it is best that you seek it from them. Spend enough time with them and get to know them at a deeper level.

I will face my troubles

Many women prefer to run away from their troubles instead of facing them. But this can be a bad thing. Just by running away from them, you cannot expect to fix them, or expect them to fix themselves. Try to remain as positive and take your troubles head on. If it is a health or, an emotional issue then have it addressed at the earliest. You will feel much better once you have the issue addressed.

I will not get angry

Stop getting angry unnecessarily. Many women feel angered just at the mention of certain words. But learn to ignore it and not have your heart skip a beat every time someone mention's your exes name or the word "divorcee". You will end up harming yourself with your anger and not anyone else. Try to remain as calm and composed as possible at all times. Say this chant out loud every time you feel like venting your anger.

I will take care of my health

Health should be given primary importance regardless of what circumstances surround you. Don't go on a binging spree and consume too much food just to get over your divorce. Promise yourself that you will only consume healthy foods and nothing else. Try to consume foods that are good for women such as fish oils and flax seeds. Make a meal plan and stick with it. Ask a friend or a relative to keep an eye on your food habits.

I will seek support

All women are super women no doubt, but even those need support in rough times. Don't refrain from seeking help from your loved ones and friends. Don't turn them away when they offer to help you. You will need all the care and support and must be open to it. You can also join a support group in your area if you wish to recover from the phase fast enough. Keep reciting this chant from time to time and reach out to others.

I will stick with my job

Some women decide to quit their job and stay at home. They assume that they need to take some time off to focus on themselves. But this is not true and it is important that the woman stay put at her job. Tell yourself that you will stick with your job, or look for a better one but not quit at any cost. Try to divert your mind from your situation as much as possible. It is important that you keep reciting this phrase every now and then.

I will look out for love

Don't stop looking out for love. Remain positive and hope for the best. You will surely find someone else who will love you and care for you. Don't go about it too fast and try to maintain a little gap between your divorce and finding someone new. Don't keep thinking that all men will turn out to be the same way. Everybody is different.

I will not pay attention to others

When you go through a divorce, there will be both good people and bad that will surround you and give away opinions. It is important that you not take the bad comments to heart. Try to remain as away from it as possible and remain happy. Keep reciting this chant and put it into practice as much as possible.

I am a strong, beautiful and independent woman

Keep reminding yourself that you are a beautiful and independent woman who does not need the support of a man to complete her. You can lead a happy life without depending on another person. Recite this chant as many times a day as possible and be happy.

These form the different positive affirmations that women going through a divorce must recite.

For college students

It is important for college students to speak a few positive affirmations before they start college. They will find it easier to settle into their new life.

<u>I am blessed to be in college</u>

Not all students have the opportunity of going to college. If you have made it, then you must be grateful for the opportunity you have received and count your blessings. Appreciate what the people in your life have done for you and given you the opportunity to go to college. Thank god for allowing you to study further and complete your education.

<u>I will not fear this new life</u>

Many students fear stepping into college as it will be radically different from school life. There will be more number of students and some bullies as well. But don't give into such fears. If you remain confident, then nobody will judge or bully you. If you enter college fearing about the repercussions then you will have trouble settling in. So try to remain as strong as possible. If you do have some sort of fear, then keep reciting this affirmation and drive that fear away.

<u>I have chosen the right major</u>

It is usually confusing to choose the major, as you will have different interests. But you must make up your mind on the best one and pursue it. Try to listen to your heart and choose the right major for yourself. Look at all the options available to you and then make your choice. Don't blindly follow what someone else is doing and carve out your own niche. After you have chosen the subject, start chanting this positive affirmation and you will begin to appreciate your choice better.

<u>I will make new study friends</u>

You must not refrain from socializing in college. There will be different types of people all of whom will bring in a different energy into your life. You must try to mingle with each one and not stick with just one group. Try creating a diverse group and remain at the helm of affairs. Remember to pick friends that are encouraging of studying and excelling academically and those that will help you organize study groups and studiously study every day.

I will excel

It is important to tell yourself that you will excel in your studies. Just making it to college is not that big of an achievement. You must supplement it with good studies and try to excel in it. This will ensure that you get a good job as well and can lead an ideal life. So think a little into the future and ensure that you maintain good grades and don't take it lightly. Keep reciting this affirmation, especially during your exams, and you will see how effective it really is. You can also write this down and paste it on your dorm/ hostel/ room wall.

I will proudly hold a degree

Just like with the other affirmations, it is important that you see into the future and think positively. So tell yourself that you will one day proudly hold a degree in your hand and show your parents that you succeeded in doing what you set out to. Try to picture your graduation where you are holding the degree in your hand and are feeling proud of the moment. And you have not only graduated but have also excelled in it and topped your class. You are receiving a thunderous applaud for your achievement.

I will not skip classes

One important affirmation to recite is "I will not skip any classes". Many students end up skipping classes when they enter college.

This is mainly owing to the freedom that is given away. Try not to do so and remain in college for the entire course of the day. Don't think attending classes will eat away into your leisure and fun time. You can continue to have fun after your classes but not during them. If you know others who are doing so, then ask them not to do it instead of following them.

I will not get into the wrong company

Getting into the wrong company is quite easy when you are in college. Maybe you have a bad roommate who is into bad habits and forcing you to get in as well or some seniors who are not ideal friends. Try to stave them off as much as possible and don't remain in their company. You can inform some of your teachers about it and get them to help you out. Try to remain as away from bad company as possible, and maintain focus on your studies. Recite this affirmation on a daily basis.

I will respect my teachers

Your teachers are your mentors and those that will impart knowledge. So it is important that you respect them and not make fun of them. Even if they are not to your liking, you must not judge them. If you don't like them then keep it to yourself, they need not know about it. Try to remain as friendly with them as possible and don't get into their bad books. You can recite this chant every now and then or write it down on a piece of paper and stick it where you can see it regularly.

<u>I will study daily</u>

It is not enough if you simply attend classes regularly. You must also study on a daily basis. Try to spend at least an hour or 2 studying whatever was taught in class. That way, you will be prepared for surprise tests and quizzes. You will not feel burdened when a big test approaches and will be ready for it. Set yourself a timer or alarm and start studying.

These form the different positive affirmations that college students need to recite to excel academically.

For new job

Many people feel nervous while starting a new job. It will be a different environment and they will have to change certain habits. Let us look at some positive affirmations for such people to take up.

I'm fully prepared for the interview

The very first step is to do well in job interviews. When you wish to change your job, you need to do well in the interviews. It should not be mediocre or satisfactory, it should be great! So prepare yourself for an interview first and tell yourself that you are fully prepared for an interview. Go to it feeling confident and having full knowledge of what might be asked and how you must reply to it.

<u>I love my new job</u>

Once you get placed at a new place, you must start loving your job. I know it is tough to fall in love with your work place but it has to be done if you wish to excel in your job. Keep repeating this positive affirmation and try to love whatever that you do at your work place. You can also type this on your cell phone or tablet and look at it every now and then to remain motivated and do your best at your work.

<u>I will make new friends</u>

A new place brings about new people. You must be prepared for it and try to be at your friendly best. Try making a new friend on a daily basis and explore the types of personalities present at your work place. Try to have a diverse friend group consisting of both men and women. Don't wrongly judge anyone and open up to each one. Avoid keeping to yourself or fearing being judged and mingle with everyone, as much as possible.

I will not complain

Don't keep complaining about your work and learn to enjoy it. Many people who join work feel like they are burdened with a lot of work, including that of others. But this might not be true and you might be feeling so owing to stress. So combat it and try to remain positive. After a while, you will start settling in and it will start getting easier for you. Say this affirmation, out loud, as soon as you get to work.

I will put in hard work

Hard work pays off extremely well. So you must try to work as hard as possible and excel at your work place. Promise yourself that you will do everything in your power to put in your best and nothing less. You will strive to be the best employee in the firm. You will not give into unnecessary pressure and do right by your talents and capacity. You must recite this chant on a daily basis and see to it that you put in sufficient hard work.

I will get a raise easily

It is not fun being stuck in the same pay scale for long. You have to strive hard to earn a raise and earn more than whatever you usually do. Promise yourself that you will put in hard work and get a raise easily. Keep reciting this affirmation every now and then and believe in it for it to come true. Don't feel bad if someone else gets a raise before you, remain positive and you will get yours as well.

I make most of my office time

Think of your time spent at office as time spent well. Avoid sitting and gossiping instead of working. You will get into trouble if you are not up to the mark. Try to remain as positive and motivated to put in your best at your work place. Tell yourself that you will perform well at your office and think of it as your prime time to focus on your job. You will realize that you are getting more work done in lesser time.

I fight thoughts of boredom

Thoughts of boredom might naturally occur to you, especially if you are stuck in a bad job. It is important that you fight these thoughts and also put an end to your frustration. You must understand that there is no escape and you have to put up with your job if you wish to make progress in life. Who knows, you might end up making enough money to have an early retirement. So recite this chant as often as possible and put an end to your feeling of boredom.

I will be up for a challenge any time!

Don't be too rigid at your workplace and be prepared for a challenge any time. Don't refuse to take up a job that is offered to you by your boss. It is best that you finish your day's work slightly early and wait for your boss to assign any new work. If you have your own work pending, then you will not be prepared to take on extra work.

I'm not worried about recession

Recession is a scary topic for many people. They think that recession will strike and they will not be left with a job. But it is extremely important to not entertain such thoughts and remain positive. Don't think the recession will strike and you will end up losing your job. Have faith in your work ability and understand the importance of not panicking unnecessarily. Believe that recession will not affect your work and you will sail through it having a steady job.

These form the different positive affirmations that you need to chant when you wish to start a new job.

For pregnant women

Pregnancy is a special time for any woman, but there are several challenges that it brings along and it is important for the woman to prepare for all of these challenges.

<u>I will take good care of myself</u>

It is important that the pregnant woman take good care of her body. She has to care for another living person inside her and cannot take her health lightly. She should be asked to recite this phrase as many times in a day as possible. Right from food intake to maintaining herself physically, the woman must do all the right things for herself and her to be born child. If she comes under any stress then she should be reminded to recite this as many times as possible.

<u>I am a strong woman</u>

When a woman is pregnant, she will go through a lot of mental and emotional upheavals, so it is important to remain strong to sail through all of it. The woman should recite, "I am a strong woman" as many times as possible and see to it that she feels strong emotionally and physically. She should be reminded how important it is to remain positive all through the journey and the only way that can happen is if she is positive.

I will have a smooth journey

The woman needs to carry a baby inside her for 9 whole months and it will not always be an easy task. However, with the help of positive affirmations such as these, the woman can make it an easy sailing experience for herself. Constantly telling herself that she will have a smooth journey will help her remain calm and also be happy. She will spend her 9 months enjoying herself and not worry about what is to come.

My baby and I will bond well

It is extremely important for a woman to develop a loving bond with her child and vice versa. I know it comes about naturally, but it can be heightened through the power of positive affirmations. The woman must recite this and develop a deep bond with her baby. Speaking to the baby while it is inside the stomach goes a long way in encouraging the child to start developing a deep and loving bond with the mother. It will further help if the father of the baby also talks to the child.

I love my pregnant body

Many women start feeling awkward or worry that they will lose their body's shape when they are pregnant. But it is important to not think that way and love our pregnant body. Yes, it will be quite difficult as you will put on a lot of weight and also have to deal with nausea and swollen ankles, but all this is a part and parcel of pregnancy and it is best to not care for these too much and accept and embrace them. You must think of your pregnant body as being uniquely beautiful, especially because there is another life that is living inside you now. Don't be too hard on yourself and start enjoying the changes that occur in your body.

I will sail through my labor

Many pregnant women start thinking about their labor pains and feel panicky. This will only worsen the woman's mental and emotional state. So it is important for the woman to not think about her labor until the last trimester. Even then, she must only think of how smooth it will be and how giving birth will turn out to be the most enjoyable experience of her life.

My baby knows I love him/ her

It is important for a mother to be to have certain assurances when it comes to her bonding and relationship with her baby. She must tell herself that her baby loves her just as much as she loves her baby. The kind of confidence that this type of positivity imparts to both the mother and the child is simply impeccable. The child will truly love the mother to a very large extent. The mother will remain motivated to enjoy her pregnancy and do all the right things towards making it easy for herself and her baby.

I will embrace my contractions

Contractions are what scare many pregnant women. They fear the very process of giving birth and start thinking how painful it actually will be. But it is important to embrace the contractions and not allow it to get the best of your fears. Try to remain positive all throughout your pregnancy and tell yourself that it will be okay. In fact, it will be more than okay and you will have a great time giving birth to your lovely child.

I had an amazing birthing experience

It always pays to speak positively about a future event. The mother to be should be asked to say, "I just had an amazing birthing experience". This will actually force the ideal situation to come through. The woman must visualize the situation vividly and convince herself that everything is going as per plan and in fact, much better.

I have brought my healthy baby home

The next positive affirmation to swear by is, "I have bought my healthy baby home". As you know, it pays to speak positively about a future event. The woman must see that she has bought a healthy baby home if she wants to experience it. She will have to say it repeatedly and ensure that it turns into a reality. She must visualize herself bringing home a healthy and strong baby with her from the hospital.

I will be a great mother

Carrying the baby for 9 months is not the only task that the woman has to care about; she must promise herself to be the best mother to her baby. She must be hands on with the baby and try to be there for each of her baby's needs.

These form some of the best positive affirmations that a pregnant woman must tell herself.

For miscarriages

Many women suffer miscarriages as it is out of their control. It is no doubt a very harrowing time and it is important that the woman maintain calm composure at such a trying time. Positive affirmations will help the woman sail through the tough phase.

I will overcome this

The very first positive affirmation to swear by is "I will overcome this". No phase in life lasts long and it will pass very soon. You must maintain a calm composure and not worry about whatever just happened. This positive affirmation has helped many people withstand a bad phase in their life. Keep telling yourself that this phase will pass very soon and it will be all right in no time at all.

It was God's will

Many women take it on themselves and blame themselves for whatever went wrong. But this is not right. Don't blame yourself. Tell yourself that it is in god's will that something like that happened. It is obvious that you will also be quite angry with God for whatever happened, but tell yourself that everything happens for a reason and that this will pass. In fact, the more you thank God, the more strength that you develop to sail through such a phase.

I will have a healthy baby next

Positive affirmations are all about wishing for the best. So tell yourself that you will have a healthy baby next. You will not be bothered by the bad experience and will look forward to a positive life. You will get pregnant again and have a healthy baby. You must also visualize yourself having a healthy baby. See that you are pregnant and glowing again and have given birth to a healthy baby. You will start feeling better in no time at all.

I know I cannot control everything

You must tell yourself that you really cannot control everything in your life. Even if it feels like you have everything under your control, there might be something that will go wrong. So don't go too hard on yourself and tell yourself that it will be all right. Even if you had the power to control it, something or the other would have still gone wrong. So stop thinking of whatever has passed and look towards the future.

I will support my partner

Many times, women don't realize that they aren't the only ones who have been affected by the news of miscarriage negatively and that their partner too, needs care and support. Try to be available for your partner as much as possible. Don't make it just about yourself and help your partner recuperate from the situation. The two of you must love and support each other through the tough times. Say this positive affirmation in the morning and try to check on your partner regularly, just as he would check on you.

I will regain my health

Health generally takes a back seat when women go through a miscarriage, as they will start worrying in excess. But it is important to not worry so much and promise yourself to regain your health. Tell yourself that you will start eating and exercising regularly so that you regain your health. Try to not stress yourself out anymore and keep checking your weight. Don't let yourself go. The faster that you regain your health, the better your chances of getting pregnant again so, try to remain as healthy as possible.

I will make all the right choices

Promise yourself that you will make all the right lifestyle choices for yourself. Don't get into any bad habits just to get over a bad phase. You need to concentrate on your health and ensure that you completely recover mentally, emotionally and physically from a bad experience. Try to focus on the future and how you will turn over the bad incident.

I will never give up

Tell yourself that you will never give up on your efforts and will conceive a healthy baby one day or the other. Keep trying and don't think something will go wrong again. Remain positive and ensure that you are doing all the right things.

I know now that a star up there belongs to me!

This is the last affirmation and will help you remain positive for life. It is a popular belief that those that don't make it on earth, turn into a star. You must think of your unborn child the same way. Think that a star up there is your child and is looking down upon you. You will feel much better by believing in this positive affirmation.

These form the different positive affirmations that you need to tell yourself when you have gone through a miscarriage.

For people getting married

Marriage is a big step for anyone. The person has to start caring for two people and that is quite a change. So it is important to recite a few positive affirmations, which will help the person sail into a married life.

I have found my soul mate

The first positive affirmation to start with is, "I have finally found my soul mate". As you know, just the thought of living with your soul mate can make you happy. When the time comes to settle down with them, you must remind yourself that the person you have chosen is extremely special and will keep you happy for life. You will feel extremely happy going into the relationship and embrace it better.

I am ready to settle down

Many people suffer jitters when it comes to getting married and settling down. These jitters can worsen when the time to walk down the aisle approaches. So it is important to tell yourself that you are ready to settle down with your partner. There is a difference between saying it and feeling it. Don't worry if you don't feel it the first few times but after a while you definitely will feel it.

I will have a dream wedding

The stress of a wedding can get to the calmest of persons. They will start worrying about their wedding day, the venue, the food etc. and start getting cold feet. But stressing out is never a good idea and will make you feel extremely tired on your wedding day. To help you in this department, it is best that you keep telling yourself how you will "have a dream wedding". This positive affirmation will help you have a smooth sailing marriage day. Don't overthink about the D-day and allow it to take its course.

I am really excited about marriage

Marriage means the beginning of a new phase in your life. You will go through a lot of new experiences. You must be prepared for all of it. You must feel really excited about your marriage and tell yourself that you are fully prepared for anything that your marriage puts forth. You must embrace the experience and enjoy yourself right from the very beginning.

I will love and respect my partner

When a wedding takes place, it refers to the coming together of two distinct individuals. Even if the two of you share some commonalities, you must respect and love your partner unconditionally. You must believe that your partner is the most unique person in the world and that you will accept them in whatever way. Respect them in all their decisions and tell yourself that you will trust your partner and not unnecessarily question them and their decisions.

My life is much better after marriage

Just like any other situation, you must tell yourself that your life will improve post marriage. Try to visualize how your life will be post your wedding. How you and your partner are leading happy lives and the two of you are basking in each other's company. Tell yourself that all your problems will now be shared and your happiness doubled. Your life will be extremely smooth sailing and you will have an enjoyable time with your partner.

I will uphold its sanctity

Marriage is a very sacred institution. You must promise to uphold its sanctity and do right by your partner at all times. Tell yourself that you will uphold the sanctity of your marriage and not do things that will violate it. You must be as loyal to your partner as possible and not indulge in activities that will hurt your partner. It is important that you recite this affirmation as many times as possible, especially during the very initial stages of your marriage. Remain as loyal and loving towards your partner and don't do anything that will hurt their feelings.

I will protect my partner

You must always try to protect your partner from negative influences. Whether it is others or something that bothers your partner, you must try to stave it off and not allow it to affect your partner negatively. Be by your partner through thick and thin and ensure that you are doing everything in your power to protect your partner.

I will love through sickness and health

This is a vow that most people say while getting married but it is seen that not everybody upholds it. But you must promise both yourself and your partner that you will support and love them through their tough times. Try to remain as positive and wish for all the best.

It's a lifetime choice

When you decide to get married, it is a lifetime choice and not something that you take up momentarily. Tell yourself that it is a lifetime choice that you have made and are going to stick with your partner for life. Of course it is impossible to predict the future but you must remain as positive about it as possible.

Chapter 2

Some Important Affirmations In Brief

Entrepreneur's Affirmations

<u>I attract opportunities</u>

An entrepreneur should always look for opportunities in anything that he or she does. In fact, finding and exploiting a good opportunity is what will help both budding and established entrepreneurs get the most out of their business. With this positive affirmation it will be easier for the entrepreneur to attract a lot of opportunities towards himself or herself and have the chance to grow their business by leaps and bounds. It is ideal to recite this over and over again until it starts to work on the psyche and the person is able to invite and identify good opportunities in life.

I succeed easily

Success is the biggest achievement for an entrepreneur. It is in fact the primary goal pf a business and something that will help the person remain positive and keep going. In order to bring about immense success into the workspace the entrepreneur must recite, "I succeed easily". This is sure to make the journey smooth and the person will have the chance to succeed with ease. It is vital for success to come through easily and must not be an elusive asset. Once success starts to role in the entrepreneur will grow confident and start reciting this chant to keep the successful streak going.

Positivity is me

The work environment has all types of people and there can be those who will be quite negative. These people are capable of affecting even the strongest mindset and will stop at nothing to turn others negative. This should be best countered with positivity. Positivity is for all those that seek to counter the negativity that surrounds them. An entrepreneur cannot just break free from the shell of negativity but also invite a lot of positivity just by encouraging these positive thoughts and acting on it. The entrepreneur is required to equate himself with positivity and think that he is positivity personified.

I am on top of my game

Being on top of one's game is the gold standard for any entrepreneur. It means a lot to be the market leader and is sure to get the entrepreneurs hopes high that one day he will be the world leader. In order for this to come about the person needs to recite this quote over and over again. He or she will successfully overcome all the hurdles and move to the top of the market with ease. It is essential for them to believe that it will happen for them and they are sure to realize their dreams and attain success.

I am result oriented

For any business, it is important to be results oriented. Positive results are what will help them move forward and grow bigger. The entrepreneur is supposed to be result oriented in order to move forward. He or she has to believe that positive outcomes will come through with all the effort that is put into their business. Reciting I am result oriented will make it easier for them to see these results and they will have the chance to progress in life.

I love what I do everyday

Monotony can set in at any time for anyone. This is especially true for entrepreneurs, as they do not have much choice in moving from one job to another. Here, it becomes important to love their job and look at each day's work as an interesting aspect of life.

Only then will they have the chance to continue on with their journey and keep aiming higher and higher in order to make the most out of their business. Reciting this chant every now and then, especially after getting into the office will help the entrepreneur in a big way.

<u>I am a role model for victory</u>

There is nothing like reaffirming your position in life. If you remind yourself how successful you are and how easily you attain victory then you will know your true authority. You will look at the number of people that look up to you and how many actually see you as their role model. You will feel extremely joyous and wish to keep up with the work that you are doing. You have to remain affirmative and continue to inspire others and make sure that they are following in your footsteps.

<u>I am always optimistic</u>

There is nothing like optimism for an entrepreneur. Regardless of owning a big industry or running a small firm, optimism is key for all types of businessmen. In fact, optimism will only help the person attain better results and they will have the chance to land better deals just by being positive. This chant is sure to increase the entrepreneur's potential.

<u>Every day brings me prosperity</u>

Prosperity should always be in motion and never should it stagnate. It should flow into a person's life like water and the best way to make this happen is by chanting this quote. It is possible for the person to allow prosperity to flow through and make everyday a special day. Even if it is a matter of a small profit, it is still an achievement and a mark of prosperity.

<u>My financial abundance is my biggest asset</u>

For an entrepreneur, his or her financial abundance is their biggest asset. They will feel proud of what they have and remain positive about their business. Reminding yourself about your financial abundance and how hard you have worked for it will help you invite more financial security. You must recite this quote over and over again and look at your finances as your biggest asset.

Rough Patch Affirmations

<u>I know it will pass</u>

Going through a rough patch can be extremely tough for any human being. But it is the law of nature to have phases of ups and downs. You cannot control these things and must remain positive through it. You have to be confident that it will pass. Change is the law of nature and nothing remains the same all through out. You have to tell yourself that it is only a matter of time when this bad phase passes and you will return to normalcy. You will not even remember the phase after a few years even if it was extremely bad.

I can do it

There is nothing like a positive affirmation to get you through a tough time. Just telling yourself that you can do it and ride through the bad phase will help you get over it. That is all that it takes to ride over a bad phase. Your mental strength is your biggest asset and you have the capacity to get over anything in life. Keep saying I can do it over and over again and you are sure to ride the tide. The bad phase will pass at rapid speed and you will not even feel the damage it caused.

Tomorrow will be brighter

Remember that there is always a tomorrow. This means that you have the chance to look forward to better things. Those who think positively will only invite positivity. That is the very basics of positive affirmations. So just by inviting a better tomorrow you have the chance to converting it into a reality. So tell yourself that no matter what happens at the end of the day today, tomorrow is always a brighter and better day. Not only will you set things right but a lot of positivity will flow in and better your life.

Positivity is my only mindset

Your mindset will change from time to time and if it is positive now, it will turn negative later. But through all this, you have to try and have a consistent positive mindset all through out. There is just no scope for negativity in positive affirmations. You have to be determined to remain positive all throughout. In fact, it should be your default mindset and something that will automatically come about even without you trying hard to turn it on. It should be your mind in auto pilot mode.

My destiny is unfolding

Whenever you hit a rough patch, tell yourself that your destiny is unfolding. You must have heard of the adage everything happens for a reason. So if something is happening in your life then it only means that it was meant to be. There is a reason why things are happening the way they are in your life. So you have to remain positive all through out it and look for the light at the end of the tunnel. You are sure to get out of the tunnel if you remain positive otherwise you will only end up walking in lop.

I am happy no matter what life brings

You are the sole proprietor of your happiness and there is nobody or nothing that can influence it. This means that only you can affect your happiness and not anybody else. Even if life throws the worst at you, you have to face it with a positive attitude. Only then will it not affect your happiness. Your happiness is your core value and there should be nothing that can affect it. No matter how bad the situation gets you have to remain happy and positive all throughout and not have anything affect it regardless of whether it is people, situations, circumstances etc.

I will learn from all experiences

All the experience that you gain in this world is you learning curve. You have to be ready to learn from everything that comes your way and think of it as a teacher. You have to look for the positive in positive situations no doubt but you need to look for positives in negative situations as well. As long as you get to take away positivity from a situation you will have the chance to get over it with ease.

I will forgive everyone

As was mentioned before, you are the sole authoritarian of your happiness and nobody can affect it. If someone has hurt you then it means you have allowed yourself to get hurt. If you put up a strong façade then nobody can penetrate it. Even if someone is trying to break in and affect you then they will not succeed. Even if they do it means that you have decided to take down that wall yourself. So holding a grudge against them is useless. You have to learn to forgive and forget. You can easily forgive someone and move on. The more you forgive someone the better that you handle the situation.

I will confidently move on

Never get hung over someone and have the confidence that you will move on confidently. This type of positive thinking will save you from heartbreaks. Remember that no one person is worth crying over and you have to love yourself more than anybody else. Once you give yourself more respect you will easily move on from anyone and any situation. It is up to you to forget about someone and what you did and confidently move past a situation. Say to yourself that you will confidently move on and you will realize that it will happen for sure.

I will be a better person

Many times, you might end up wronging others. But that is also a learning curve for you. You have to tell yourself that you will become a better person and make sure that you don't repeat the same mistakes over and over again. Have a positive outlook towards life and see each and every situation as a means for you to learn from and move past.

Sex Affirmations

<u>I love sex and it pleasures me</u>

Sex is a pleasurable experience for everybody. But there can be some who look at it through the eyes of guilt or shame. This can be a big problem as not only is sex important for the body but also for a relationship to remain strong. You have to tell yourself that you love sex and it pleasures your body. This means that it is a natural desire to be pleased and you are only helping your body get what it deserves. You have to love sex in order to enjoy it and leave all your inhibitions behind.

<u>I am a sexually confident person</u>

There is nothing like sheer confidence and your sexual confidence will be the biggest turn on for your partner. Having regular sex will help you get acquainted with your body and the different areas that pleasure you. Once you have the confidence of knowing your body thoroughly you will turn extremely desirable and your partner will count his/ her blessings for having you in their life. So chant this several times to up your confidence level and get your partner to fall in love with you and your body all over again.

I love to experiment with sex

Sex should never be the same thing and you must change it up from time to time in order to enjoy it better. For this, you have to experiment with sex and not stick to doing the standard old things. Try and change it up from time to time and don't be afraid to go bold. Tell yourself that you will confidently experiment for sex for yourself and your partner's pleasure. You will only cause the pleasure to heighten and your confidence level will rise up.

I have amazing sexual powers

Everybody has a unique body and different personalities. You have to tell yourself that you have an amazing body and are capable of unleashing sexual powers. These powers make you unique and give you the chance to pleasure your partner to the highest extent. It is like a super power that you have and you only unleash it in bed. This will not only up your confidence but pave the way for a heightened sexual experience.

My partner loves being with me

For any sexual experience to feel complete there has to be an emotional connection. This means that you have to have a partner who loves being with you. Many times, we end up doubting our own worth and wonder if our partners are really interested in being with us. But this should be converted into a confident thought and you must tell yourself that your partner loves being with you. There is a reason for him or her to come to you for bodily pleasure and that reason is the love they have for you and your body.

I am blessed to have great sex

Sexual pleasure is a 2 way street. You have to enjoy yourself in order for your partner to enjoy it. Once you start you will feel blessed to have a partner who is capable of pleasuring you. You will have the confidence to do better each time and reward your partner for being in your life. Even if you don't have a steady partner, you must feel blessed for having great sex come your way and think of it as a blessing for doing good things.

I am grateful for my sex

There are many people out there who are still in search of a good sexual experience. It is like the experience eludes them and they can never find a partner who can satisfy them. That should not be you. You have to be grateful for the sexual experience that you are getting in life in order to keep it coming. You must never complain about anything lest you wish to affect the flow of things in life. If you are getting a lot of pleasure in bed then allow it to continue and be grateful for it coming your way.

Men love my body (for women)

Women can have a lot of inhibitions and are afraid of disclosing their bodies to men. They wonder if they will be appreciated or the men will love their bodies. But you need positive affirmation in order to get men to love your bodies. Don't even think of speaking about your flaws, as your partner does not need to know about them or see them. If you know something, then keep it to yourself and don't go around speaking about it. Give your partner the chance to form an opinion and don't try to influence it just to get something out of the way. Remain confident and don't speak about anything that you think will be a problem for your partner.

Women love my body (for men)

It is a misconception that men don't have inhibitions in regard to their bodies. They also feel the same way about their bodies as women do and might be insecure about certain aspects. Again, don't disclose any secrets in regard to your body. It is up to your partner to form an opinion and you must not influence it. It will stop being a natural process and end up being an influenced one. So don't get over enthusiastic and start pointing at flaws on your body. Tell yourself that women love my sexy body and up your confidence level.

I am satisfied with my performance

Always be satisfied with your performance in bed. Remember that you perform for your pleasure and it takes top priority. You wish to satisfy your partner no doubt but it is not something that you have to prioritize. It is about pleasuring your body and if you concentrate on doing that then you will automatically pleasure your partner's body as well.

Affirmations for Children

I am good with math, science, French etc.

Children's minds are naïve and you have to help in molding it the right way. You have to teach your children positive affirmations, which will help in creating a positive mindset. Start by teaching them to recite affirmations in regard to their studies. Tell them to chant I am good in math or science or language and all their subjects. This will give them the confidence to do their best and attain a lot of success in their studies. This is especially useful for those subjects, which the child finds difficult and you have to boost their confidence by getting them to chant this phrase.

I am a fast learner

For any child, learning new things is the most important part of growing up. So getting them to say "I am a fast learner" will help them learn new things at a rapid pace. They have to believe it and chant it and use it as their mantra to lean things faster. This can be at school or college or even co curricular such as swimming, dancing, singing etc. Getting them to learn things faster will not only up their confidence but they can learn many things within a short time frame.

I always speak the truth

It is important to imbibe core values right from a young age. It is never too early to teach children important values and the earlier you start the better. Teach them to recite I always speak the truth. This will help them stick with this principle and never lie no matter what the circumstances. They will have this chant come into their mind when they are faced with a situation and they will choose to stick with it instead of opposing it. So you will help your child speak the truth at all times and not lie their way through life.

God protects me

Many children have an inherent fear. They are young and are not sure how to go about their lives. They will have their parents' support no doubt but will need a reaffirmation every time. For this, you can get him or her to say that god protects me. This will help them remain confident and they will not fear life. They will go about it confidently knowing that there is someone above them who is looking at their every move and protecting them from any sort of bad influence.

I am my first friend

This is an important positive affirmation for a child to develop. Self-confidence and esteem are extremely important for everybody and it is vital that the child start right from a young age. The child must be taught to respect himself or herself first. Ask them to think of themselves as their first and best friends. Although they will have other friends, they must consider themselves as their closest friends.

I will help others

Helping others will help your child's character to develop. Not only will he or she learn to help those in need but also understand the importance of getting in return whatever is offered to others. They will learn to give and take respect as well. They must be told to not care who the person in need is and jump into action to help them. They should also be taught to thank the person that helped them out when they were in need of assistance.

I always forgive

Forgetting a bad incident is easy but forgiving the wrong doer is not. So it is important that the child be taught to forgive and forget. It is always difficult to do so but needs to be done as holding a grudge for long is not always the best choice. Teach them to forgive someone despite being wronged. Children of young ages will often make mistakes and your child should be taught to remain prepared for a fight or any such incident and not take it too much to heart. Once it passes, it is best to move on from it.

I'm a good influence

This affirmation is important to all those children that have younger siblings. Setting a good example to other siblings is as important as being a good brother or sister. Teach the older child about the importance of being a good person and setting an example to his or her younger siblings. Tell them how they will be looked up to and made into a role model. Reciting this affirmation every morning will help them do all the right things through the day. They will also feel proud for having done the right thing for themselves and their siblings.

I will remain safe

Teach your child the importance of safety. Being safe is always important for any human. Tell them how they should safeguard themselves and others around them. It is important to be physically safe and also not entertain strangers. Teach them to remain aware of everything around them at all times. React on time and do things that will keep them safe.

Nothing is impossible

Children should be taught that nothing in this world is impossible. If they put their mind to it then everything can be made possible. Tell them how important it is to pursue their dreams and look at every task as a possibility. You must ask them to recite this daily and set themselves daily goals. The more they achieve the more they believe in it. So keep them motivated to give their best in everything that they do.

I wake up with a smile

The first few seconds of waking up are the most important times of the day. The mood that persists during this time is what will remain all through the day. So teach your child to wake up with a smile every morning. This will ensure that the child is happy all through the day. You can ask them to recite it while going to bed and also paste a picture, which provokes them to break into a smile. You must also greet your child with a wide grin in the morning and encourage them to do the same with others.

I love my parents

All children need to develop a special bond with their parents. For this, you must ask them to say, "I love my parents". The more they say it, the better connected that they feel with their parents. Teach them the importance of loving someone unconditionally. They will start appreciating others, especially their parents and everything that they do for them. They will also do their best to keep their parents happy and satisfied.

I respect elders

It is vital to respect all elders. Some children will not realize its importance unless they are told why it is key to love and respect elders around them. Be it their teachers or other elders that cross their paths, it is vital to love and respect them. Ask them to recite this every now and then and see to it that they respectfully listen to what elders have to say to them.

I do not fight

Fighting is not a healthy habit for anyone to develop. You must teach your children the importance of not fighting and remaining calm no matter what the circumstance. If they fight now, it won't be long before they start getting into physical brawls, so it is important to teach them not to pick fights with other children.

I love my friends

Having good peers and friends is vital for all children. The friendships that they make when they are young are what will mold their character. This means that they have to help them establish a strong bond with a few of their best friends. You have to teach them the importance of having good friends and tell them to recite I love my friends which will help them establish a strong relationship. Even if they have fights they will know to respect their friends and do things that are right for each other.

I am a good listener

Children can get restless and not want to listen to others especially those that they think bore them. But only a good listener will be able to progress in life. Those who are restless will have to work with half knowledge, which is dangerous as you know and so, it is best to get your child to become a good listener. Ask them to chant this several times a day and turn into a good listener. They will keenly listen to everything that others have to say and equip themselves with enough and more knowledge to operate smoothly in this world.

I am beautiful from the inside out

Body image is a big thing for children and although they will not expressly say it out loud they will have a lot of inhibitions. This might be because of what they get to hear from classmates and their peers. So right from a young age you have to teach them the positive affirmation that they are beautiful from the inside out. Get them to chant, "I am beautiful from the inside out" which will help them love themselves better. It will be very difficult for an outsider to affect their thinking if they have been taught to appreciate their body and you will help them remain safe from any negative impressions for life.

I will make dreams come true

Everybody dreams about big things right from a young age. But not all get to realize them. In fact, only a handful have the chance to translate their dreams into reality. But by consistently reminding oneself about them and believing in it can make the journey more plausible. For this, ask your child to recite, "I will make my dreams come true". This will allow them to pursue their dreams and make sure that they are realized. They will work hard towards it and find that it is progressively getting easier.

I love to exercise

Exercise is vital for all human beings. As children, they will have a lot of time and fitting in an exercise schedule will not seem difficult. So getting them to exercise by performing physical activities will help them remain healthy and fit for life. They will carry it into their adulthood and make sure that they spend enough time exercising in order to remain healthy and continue on with life full of energy and feeling fit.

<u>I eat healthy foods</u>

Just like exercising, consuming healthy and nutritious foods is also a positive affirmation. It will give them the chance to perform well at school in their school activities and also their co curricular activities. They will learn the importance of eating healthy to remain fit and healthy for long and realizing all their dreams. You also have to set an example for them and consume the best foods yourself. You can also recite the same to help them learn from you. Get them to say it when they are having the food so that they learn to associate the two and don't think of it as just a random, good chant.

Positive Affirmations for Elders

<u>I live to contribute positivity</u>

Many senior citizens will require positive affirmations to lead a normal life. One of the first and best affirmations to start with is "I live to contribute positivity". This is a chant that helps them remain positive and also spread positivity around them. It will change the outlook that they have towards life. They will remain positive and invite positive thoughts and actions. Get them to chant this at least 5 times a day and it is best done in the mornings as soon as they get up so that they start the day on a positive note.

I choose to live comfortably

Comfort is everybody's right and you have to tell the elders in your life that it is a choice that they make for themselves. So they have the right to choose how they live and if comfort is top priority then so be it. They have earned it and deserve to live comfortably. There is no point in making sacrifices any more and they can choose to live as comfortably as they like. Tell them to recite this chant so that they feel confident and it makes them feel worthwhile. It will help them lead a better life.

I am growing stronger day after day

Elders need to feel that their body is not disintegrating. The mind has enough power to undo many things including bodily functions. If they chant I am growing stronger day after day then it will only help them convert that statement into a fact. They will feel stronger and full of life. They will not get tired easily and a new lease of life will be ignited. They should be told to recite this statement every day so that they grow stronger by the day. There should be an instant increase in their confidence levels just by chanting these words.

My mentality is clear

They have to chant that their mentality is clear and they still have the capacity to make all the important decisions for life. They are not getting confused and that everything is clear to them. They should be encouraged to take up positive activities for their mind such as reading something, solving a puzzle etc. This will further boost their confidence and they will do more with their mental power. This will boost their confidence and take their mind off of unnecessary things. They have to say, "My mentality is clear and will remain that way".

I love my mature body

Body image changes when it comes to elders. They will start to look at their gray hair, their wrinkles and dark circles and their confidence will start to deteriorate. And that is not a good sign. If you are a senior citizen then look at all these signs and think of them as being a beautiful addition to your body. They are god given assets and they will only distinguish you from the others. Recite, "I love my mature body" and it is sure to help you accept the way you look and feel. If you know any senior citizens then get them to chant this.

My children and grandchildren are my strength

For any senior citizen, their children and grandchildren are their biggest assets. They impart strength and give the senior citizens the confidence to live a fuller life. Even if they stay far and you get to meet them only once in a while then you have to make the meetings count. They are your strength and you have to keep saying it to affirm it. You will carry on with life with better enthusiasm and fervor.

I will live long enough to fulfil all desires

Every body has a list of desires to fulfill in this lifetime. It is important to want to fulfil these no matter what the circumstances. It is important for senior citizens to chant, "I will live long enough to fulfill all desires". This will give them an opportunity to realize their dreams and continue to live well until all their desires have been fulfilled. Saying this every day and believing in it will only increase longevity as also make every small moment in life special. Say it at least twice a day- once in the morning and once in the evening and you will feel full of life and want to fulfill all your dreams.

I find a new purpose everyday

There should be something new to look forward to on a daily basis. Every day is a new day and it will bring me new prospects.

This should be your number one mantra for life. You have to look for a new purpose on a daily basis and not remain absorbed in something that has passed. Find your self a new thing to look forward to and you are sure to feel completely rejuvenated.

<u>I attract positive people towards me</u>

You have to recite this to make sure that you attract only positive and happy people towards you. Even if you are surrounded by a lot of negativity you are safe from it and are only entertained by the positive people that surround you. You will feel good about it and feel blessed for having good people around you who are meant to make your life worthwhile. So attract positivity towards you by reciting this positive affirmation.

<u>I love my fellow elders</u>

Everybody needs good company no matter at what stage of life they stand at. For this, you have to love your fellow elders and senior citizens. You must positively affirm, "I love my fellow elders". You must recite it over and over again and look at your friends and neighbors as your best friends.

Marriage Affirmations

<u>I love my partner</u>

This is probably the most important positive affirmation for a relationship to last. You need to love your partner deeply and say it out every now and then. In fact, you must say it in your head as often as possible in order to remind yourself that you love your partner deeply. It is a quintessential part of your life and you are only reiterating something that will help you lead a loving and caring life. You can insert the name of your partner and chant this phase in your head to derive strength from it.

I will keep him/ her happy

Happiness is the founding stone for all marriages. If you are not happy then it is not worthwhile to continue on in a relationship. For this, you have to tell yourself that you will do your best to keep your partner happy and make sure that the relationship lasts for a long time. If you expressly keep telling yourself then you will make sure that it is turned into a reality instead of just an idea that lingers around in your head. You will put in more efforts to make them happy and feel content.

I am grateful for my spouse

Every day, there are so many things that your spouse does or you and most of it goes unnoticed. But you will derive a benefit out of it and your life will turn smoother thanks to their efforts. For this, you have to be extremely grateful for their presence in your life.

You have to thank the gods for it and say it in your head to reaffirm how blessed you are to have them in your life. You will feel extremely happy when you think about your spouse and their presence in your life. So do it for your inner peace.

<u>I expressly demonstrate my love daily</u>

Demonstrating love to your loved one and partner is crucial for a marriage to go steady and last long. Simply thinking you love someone will not suffice; you have to show it to them expressly. You have to tell yourself that you will love them and kiss them every day to demonstrate your love for them. You will also hug them and show your unconditional love no matter what the circumstances. You will kiss them once in the morning and once at night to strengthen the affirmation.

<u>I have immense respect for my partner</u>

You have to respect your partner and everything that he or she does. Not respecting someone enough is a big mistake. You have to respect their choices, decisions, the work they do and everything related to them. If you do not respect then the relationship will not last long. Even if they are much younger than you and have a different set of values, you have to respect them and love their life's purpose. Don't try to stronghold their ambitions and allow them to be themselves and do what they love to. So chant this positive affirmation and intensify the respect you have towards your partner.

I will support my partner

You have to support your partner through all their ups and downs. You have to be a pillar of strength and not go missing when they need you. Many people decide to go missing which is a big mistake. You have to remain with your partner through all their trials and tribulations and be a positive influence. For this, you must recite this chant and try and be there at all times.

I will give him/ her, their space

Doubting your partner and not being supportive of their relationships will kill the relationship. You have to remain supportive and give them their rightful freedom and space. If you barge into their personal space then you will end up becoming too needy and ruin the relationship. So recite this mantra and promise yourself that you will give him or her, their personal space and not keep butting into their relationships.

I will never intentionally hurt them

This is a positive affirmation that will keep your marriage lasting forever. There are many times when out of spite you end up doing things and saying words that you don't mean and yet say it just to get even with them. But just by choosing not to do this, you can successfully prevent hurting someone unnecessary. You have to love them enough to not intentionally hurt them by saying mean things. Recite this chant in your mind and make sure you don't say or do anything out of spite.

<u>I value my marriage above all</u>

You have to give your marriage the highest priority and rank it above all. It is very important that you treat your marriage as a holy institution and respect all its values. You have to say this chant to make sure that you are treating your marriage with utmost respect and are determined to make it last. You will never break any of the vows as they are extremely important to both you and your partner and will make sure they are upheld under all circumstances.

<u>I will teach my children the same values</u>

You have to consider your children and make sure that they are getting the right impression about marriage. You have to tell yourself that you will teach them about marriage and give them the best values to adhere to. You will set an example for them. You have to recite this mantra to make sure that you actively partake in it and not merely say it to feel good about it.

Mindfulness and Inner Self

<u>I live in this moment</u>

Mindfulness is extremely important for all human beings. It is vital to live in the moment in order to increase productivity and also make the most out of life. For this, you have to live in the current moment. Tell yourself that you will live in this moment and not remain distracted. Live in it and take in the situation. Make sure you chant it and act on it simultaneously to get the most out of it.

<u>I observe everything keenly</u>

You have to tell yourself to have your eyes and ears alert and taking in everything that is happening around you. Observe every small detail in your current situation. You have to make a mental recording of it. You will feel like you are on top of the situation and being fully aware of everything around you will only help you remain confident and handle a particular situation with ease. You will not panic and have everything under your control even in the worst situations.

<u>I enjoy every second</u>

You have to enjoy each and every second of your life. Each moment is filled with passion and enjoyment. You only live only once and there should be no time to regret or repent anything. You have to be fully present in the moment and enjoy it thoroughly. Look at all of its aspects and enjoy what life has on offer for you. You will feel great and completely rejuvenated. Keep repeating this mantra in your head until you are completely aware of it and are acting on it. Don't even think of sitting and sulking over something. That is time spent badly and you will not be able to enjoy yourself. Learn to get over your past even if it involves something grave.

<u>I know exactly what is happening</u>

When you know are fully absorbed in a situation and know exactly what is happening around you, you cannot be fooled by anyone and taken advantage of. You have to tell yourself that you know exactly what is happening and it will help you snap back to a situation. You can counter any claims and remain as open to a debate at anytime, anywhere and with anyone.

<u>I will think before I leap</u>

You have to always analyze a situation from all angles before you jump to any conclusions. You have to think everything through and tell yourself that you will not jump to any conclusions. You have to think before you leap and this positive affirmation is sure to help you do all the right things at the right times. So don't jump the gun on anything and think it through before you decide to leap, you might end up embarrassing yourself and creating problems for yourself.

I fully accept all my situations

You have to have it in you to accept any situation that you are in. it is not going to be a good situation all the time but you have to be fully absorbed in a negative situation as well. It will help you do your best no matter how bad the situation has gotten. You will know exactly how to salvage it and take away an experience from it. So recite this mantra to make sure that you are prepared to take any situation head on.

I know how to tackle all my relationships

Remaining present in the moment will allow you to tackle all your relationships and give each one the same type of attention. Nobody around you will feel neglected and everybody will love the attention they are getting from you. This will cause them to impart the same type of attention to you and all your relationships will mutually strengthen.

I know the past is over

Holding on to the past is completely useless. You have to let go of the past to move forward in life. You have to tell yourself that the past is over and you are present in the moment. Your present is your biggest opportunity and you will live out each and every moment of it to enjoy it thoroughly. The past is gone for good and you have nothing to do with it anymore. Recite this mantra several times until you are sure that your mind is not reverting back to the past and you are completely over everything hat occurred in the past.

<u>I will give the current task my all</u>

You have to promise yourself that you will give your present your all and not hold back on it. Even if it is a very small task you will take it seriously and see to it that you get it done at the earliest. You will put 100% into everything and make sure that you derive maximum benefits out of it.

<u>I don't wander too far</u>

It is human to sometimes get distracted but it is up to you to decide how distracted you want to get. You have to have a mental supervisor that tells you to not get distracted and concentrate on your situation. Don't wander off too much mentally and remain as much in the moment as possible. Even if you are distracted you have to have a physical signal like the snap of your fingers to snap out of a distraction and come back to your current situation.

Inner Self

<u>I love meditating</u>

Meditation is the best way to calm yourself down and come back to the current situation. You will instantly feel relaxed and get over any of your worries and problems. By telling yourself that you love meditating you will force yourself to meditate more often. Meditation is just sitting in a quiet and calm corner and chanting something soothing by closing your eyes. You can breathe in and out deeply to make sure that your mind is drawn to your breath and the rest of the world is cut out. You must have no distractions around you including sounds, noises and other such distractions. You can have a plant in front of you and concentrate on its flowers. You have to meditate for at least 30 minutes a day and recite this chant to help you meditate every day.

<u>My inner self is calm like the sea</u>

You have to tell yourself that your inner mind is as calm as the sea. The sea is the epitome of calmness and your mind must replicate it. There are no high tides or waves that slam against the rocks. Your mind is only concentrating on remaining calm and composed and is not easily provoked or affected. You are trying your best to feel calm and composed and are not giving into any distractions that are trying to affect your inner calm.

I love to breathe deeply

Breathing deeply is the best way to calm your inner self down. You have to concentrate on your breath and consciously make an effort to breathe in and out to get your mind to calm down. It is believed that a majority of people do not breathe from their lungs and only breathe from the top of their lungs. You have to breathe in such a way that the breath rises from your stomach and again goes back to your stomach. That's how deeply you have to breathe. Recite this chant and you will be reminded to breathe in deeply every time.

I love internal and external peace

You have to be a peace loving person in order to reel in a sense of calm. This peace should be both internal and external in nature. You have to love external peace and try and remain in a non-chaotic atmosphere. Similarly, you have to create a peaceful situation internally and maintain it in order to feel relaxed. This internal peace should be a reflection of the external peace and versa. You must try and remain as calm and composed on the outside and interact with others in a calm way. The more peace loving that you are on the inside, the same will show on your outside.

My mind and body are together

The mind and the body are not two separate entities and need to be aligned in order for you to lead a healthy and happy life. If they are not connected and you are leading a chaotic life then it will be very difficult for you to remain calm. Your inner self will be in doldrums and there will be a lot of confusion. So try and align your mind, body and soul by remaining alert and looking into your internal self to make sure that there are no discrepancies between the two.

All negativity has left me

Negativity will bring you down and cause you to feel disturbed. You will not have the enthusiasm to do anything and everything will feel like a very tough task. But just by reciting, "all negativity has left me" you will have the chance to combat it and get over it. You will physically feel like all negativity has left you and you are now full of positivity. It will instantly better your life and perk up your mood. So remain positive and recite this chant to remain happy on the inside out.

I am happy with everything in life

You have to be happy and satisfied with everything that you have in life. This includes your financial assets, the relationships you have, and the kind of status you have been dealt with etc. if you remain dissatisfied then it is useless. You will never be happy. You have to learn to find happiness in all the small things in life and derive pleasures out of it. Keep chanting I am happy with everything in my life and you will truly be satisfied by it. You will not look to other things for pleasure and will make do with whatever you have.

No anxiety comes close to me

Anxiety is something that can completely ruin your state of mind. You must not get anxious no matter what the circumstances. Anxiety is both a physical and an emotional reaction to a situation and you have to beat it as much as possible. If you mentally keep chanting no anxiety can come close to me then it can be turned into a reality. You have to mean it when you say it and do your best to physically control the negative thoughts. You will succeed at keeping your anxiety at bay and have a very good chance of remaining stress free under all circumstances.

In a chaotic situation my inner self draws me in

When there is apparent chaos on the outside you have to tell yourself that your inner self will calm you down. That is a signal for your inner self to draw you in towards the calm center. You will feel completely at ease and not pay any heed to your chaotic exterior. Immediately tell yourself that your inner self is your place to turn to and all your stress will immediately disappear.

Peaceful life is my only motto

A life of peace should be your only motto. This means that you choose to live in peace and your only state of mind is to remain calm and peaceful through all of life's trials and tribulations. You will not lose your cool no matter what the circumstances and be as self absorbed and present in the current moment as possible. This mantra is sure to better your life and cause you to feel at peace.

When You Are Angry/Confused

I forgive myself for everything

When you are angry you will immediately start blaming yourself for all that has gone wrong with you. You will immediately start to pin point at all the flaws that you have and blame your situation on your stupidities. But going too harsh on yourself is not the solution. You have to remain calm and not start pointing fingers at yourself. You have to say you forgive yourself and are not interested in blaming yourself or anybody for what has happened. It has happened because of unforeseen situations and you really must not blame yourself for it. So remain calm and draw in towards your inner self and don't feel the need to blame yourself for the problem. It is one thing to lose your calm in a bad situation but using the anger to punish yourself is not necessary or acceptable.

I can control my anger

You have to have the confidence to control your anger. You must put in all efforts to control your emotional and physical state and not erupt at each and every small mishap. You have to recite this chant repeatedly to make sure that you have your anger under your control. If the situation is extremely bad then you have to recite this chant out loudly. You have to say it fast enough and can close your eyes if necessary. Your positive affirmations are supposed to be your go to mantras that you can use to remedy a tough situation and it needs to be a tool you can use to calm yourself down at any given instance.

I quickly draw in empathy

You have to empathize with others when you are angry. This will help you understand a situation from their point of view. You have to stay calm and remain as composed as possible. You must then think about the situation from the other person's point of view and develop an unbiased opinion. If you think they are right then you must immediately develop empathy towards them and try and be fair in the situation. You have to have a fair judgement and only react in a manner that is acceptable to both. You must chant this and remain prepared for such a situation.

I always apologize and feel great

There is nothing wrong in apologizing to someone. There is no room for ego when it comes to establishing a healthy relationship. You have to apologize if it is your fault and that can save you a lot of time and energy. So recite "I always apologize and feel great" which will allow you to get over a bad situation with ease. By extending a hand of friendship you can begin to control the situation. So don't feel shy or prejudiced to do whatever is the right thing to do.

I always ask for help

When you are confused and don't know what to do then you have to turn to others for advice. Asking for help is not a bad thing. You are only trying to get out of a situation and are looking for help to do so. Ask anybody that you think can help you out of the situation. Don't be prejudiced to ask someone of a lower ranking. Recite this chant and tell yourself that you will ask for help no matter what the circumstance and better your life by making it easier for yourself.

I listen patiently

When you seek advice you have to pay keen attention to it. Don't make it look like you got what you needed and have decided to walk away. You are to remain in the conversation and listen to everything patiently. Don't butt in with your opinions. Recite, "I will listen patiently" before you go and ask for the advice and the practically apply it to your situation. When you are done listening you can decide to clear any doubts and then don't forget to thank them for their advice if you wish to get good advice coming to you in the future.

I am capable of making great decisions

You need not always turn to others for advice and must evaluate a situation thoroughly before going to someone for help. If you are capable of making a good decision, then go with it. Don't seek someone's approval if you are confident about your decisions. If you have the habit of asking others then break the habit now.

Recite this chant and increase your confidence in making your own wise decisions. You have to recite it once in the morning as soon as you wake up and then several times when you have to make an important decision.

<u>I never give up</u>

You must never give up on your situation and remain persistent until you get what you set out to find. If the situation gets a bit out of hand then you can choose to take a back seat and view the situation from an outsider's point of view and try to solve it. If you jump into a situation too early without understanding where it is headed then you might have problems solving the problem and might also give up on the situation. So instead you must focus on solving the issue in an orderly fashion and be done with it at the earliest.

<u>I remain composed when confused</u>

When you are confused you need to remain composed. If you allow your thoughts and feelings to go haywire then it will only worsen the situation. So remain calm and composed instead of furthering your confusion. If you think you are getting confused then close your eyes and draw into your inner self. Don't look outward for help and concentrate on your calm inner being. You will quickly calm down and your mind will start to clear out.

Recite a positive affirmation like "I can do it" and then look at the situation again. You will notice that your confusion has vanished and a clear solution lies in front of you.

<u>I know to solve my inner conflicts</u>

When it comes to conflicts, they are not always external in nature. They can be internal as well. For this, you should know how to solve your inner conflicts. Your inner conflicts are, in fact; worse as you have to solve it yourself and cannot enlist someone else's help. So have confidence in yourself and have a lot of control over your inner self. Don't allow it to get the best of you and exercise as much control over it as possible.

When You Want to Lose Weight

<u>I want to be healthy</u>

Weight loss is a very tough thing to deal with, as it is a major physical modification. It is easier to set goals than to actually achieve them. When you wish to lose weight you have to have a set of positive affirmations that will make your job easier. You have to start by chanting, "I want to be healthy". When you look around you and see many people who are leading a great life wowing to being healthy, you will obviously want to have the same for yourself. In order to make this a possibility you have to keep chanting this phrase and remain positive about the outcome for your weight loss.

I love exercising

Exercising is probably the biggest problem that you will face when trying to lose excess weight. But you have to muster up the courage and confidence to set a goal and achieve it within a said time frame. For that, you have to develop a love for exercising. Wake up every day feeling good about your body and chant, "I love exercising". This will have to be played in your mind until you begin your work out and are done with it for the day. Only if you say it out loud will you be able to keep going and with time, exercising will turn into an indispensable part of your every day routine.

I am approaching my ideal weight

You have to have the confidence that your body is finally losing excess weight and you are approaching your ideal weight. This ideal weight is what you have set for yourself and should vary from month to month. So say you wish to lose 4 pounds a month. Every day you have to tell yourself that your body is heading towards that weight. Your mind will actually help your body out and make it burn more calories a day to attain your monthly weight loss goal.

I remain active always

You have to remain active at all times in order to lose weight rapidly. If you think just by sweating it out in the gym you will be able to lose your weight then you are wrong. You have to make small changes like taking the stairs or cycling to work and running your own errands. All this is only possible if you ask yourself to remain active at all times and follow on a plan to be as physical as possible. Make sure you have a schedule in place and check the tick boxes on a daily basis.

My metabolism is great

Your metabolism plays a key role in helping your body remain fit. If it is slow then you will start piling on weight. For this reason, you have to tell yourself that your metabolism is great and you have the capacity to lose weight easily. The more you keep saying this to yourself the better your metabolism will be. If you are eating right and exercising well enough then there is no reason for your metabolism to be slow and your mental make up will only further better it.

I will treat my body to healthy foods

Food and diet plays an important role during weight loss. You have to eat all the right foods in all the right amounts to lose excess weight. These foods need to be healthy and nutritious. You have to tell yourself that you will treat your body to healthy foods and will not eat things that are unhealthy. This means that you will not expose your body to things that are harmful to it. You will put in extra efforts to subject it to good food that you will prepare yourself. You are losing weight because you love your body and want it to have the best experience in the world.

I will chew food down properly

You have to chew down food properly in order for it to get digested properly. When it digests properly it helps your metabolism. Your liver will have the chance to break down the complex compounds easily and throw all the junk out. If the compounds are too tough to break down then the junk will start looming in your body. That is not something you want happening. For this, you have to chew your food down and constantly tell yourself to do so. You have to chew each and every morsel down. Ideally, you have to spend 30 minutes eating each meal.

With every new step I feel lighter

Think of each of your steps as a weight loss exercise. You have to take short strides and make them rapid. You have to tell yourself that you feel lighter with each subsequent step and your body is losing fat. Your mental make up will help your body feel lighter and better.

I feel healthy from my head to toe

When you are losing weight you have to tell yourself that your every move is making you healthy from your head to your toe. This means that you are feeling better with each subsequent step. Right from the top of your head to your toes each and every organ is feeling massaged and relaxed. All your organs are healthy and fresh, oxygenated blood is flowing throughout your entire body. You are now completely rejuvenated and your mind, body and soul are all fully aligned.

I love my body no matter what

This is an affirmation that will allow you to love your body no matter what the circumstances. Even if you are losing weight at a slow pace or having a few hurdles, you have to perk yourself up by saying that you will effectively deal with all your issues and solve your weight loss problem in due time. In the meanwhile, you will love and admire your body and love it cell to cell.

I will beat all stress

Stress is a major cause of concern for many people. It is important that the person stop worrying about stress and focus more on leading a healthy life. Tell yourself daily that you will put an end to the stress in your life. You will completely root it out and not allow it to affect your negatively.

There are a thousand and one ways to make things happen in your life but whether you are ready to admit it or not, all of these involve the Law of Attraction. The small child who wishes for a gift for Christmas and then receives it does so not because his parents are wealthy, but because he is able to envision owning that particular thing which makes him very happy indeed. The lottery winner who won millions actually had the amount of that win on a piece of paper under her pillow and won it. Why? Because she believed in her win. She knew that it was going to happen and used the Law of Attraction to make it happen.

The Law of Attraction is so powerful that people have built their lives on it. People who believed in their ideas and ideals regardless of criticism are now multi-millionaires because they didn't let other people's disbelief get in the way of what they were aiming to achieve. They continued to believe in their ideas and ideals and these proved, time and time again to be very powerful ideas that turned them into multi-millionaires against all the odds of other people's disbelief.

Let's face it, if you are going to think in a negative and miserable way, you are going to be negative and miserable and all that you will bring to your life will be negative. You must know people like that. They are the ones that people avoid inviting to parties. They are the ones that see the dark side of everyone's personality and are happy to share it with you. They thrive on misery. Make a difference to your life by learning all about using the Power of Attraction and whenever you think a negative thought, look at it from another angle which is positive and it is life-changing.

Chapter 3

Tips and Tricks

Affirmations are an integral component for manifesting whatever it is you want in your life. If you want riches, affirming that riches belong to you and are simply awaiting to receive allows you to start vibrating the right kind of energy to attract riches your way. You could say you are going to fake it till you make it. Anything is possible if you are fully aware of the vibrational zone you need to be in order to attract certain things into your life. With that knowledge, it is easier for you to displace your thoughts (vibrational frequency) with the desired vibrational frequency, since this will allow you to manifest whatever it is you want instantly. For this to happen in your life, there can be no doubt; you must have 100% belief that whatever you want to happen in your life will take place exactly as you want it.

You don't need to ask or know how it will work; just ask, believe, wait and receive, as you consciously stay alert in your environment for the manifestation of whatever you want to happen. Your baseline thought vibrations (the things that you subconsciously believe in) will often determine whether your affirmations will manifest in your life. For instance, if you are diagnosed with a terminal disease, affirming that you are healed and the subsequent belief that your healing has been manifested will be enough to facilitate your healing. Don't just say it and expect it to work if you are harboring deep-rooted doubts, since the thoughts you experience when doubtful ensure that you will be vibrating the things that you don't want in your life. In this case, it is death from terminal illness.

Find a way of converting your negative energy into positive energy through changing your focus. Start focusing on the things that you really want. That way, you will start vibrating your desired energy, thus attracting the energy that matches your vibrational frequency. This technique is extremely potent and there are many testimonials available that stress on how positive affirmations have helped them sail through the troubles in their life. So how do you get to a point of manifesting what you want instantly through your affirmations? There are some simple steps that will help you prepare yourself properly if you are to manifest whatever you want in your life instantly.

Before you can get to the point of receiving instant manifestations of whatever you want to happen in your life, you need to change your personal vibration and your environmental vibration. This could simply be described as trying to find your path of least resistance if you are to fully experience your desired manifestations.

Are you among those who find it easier to attract undesirable manifestations in your life even when you have tried to affirm certain things in your life? Do you know why this happens? It is because when you have negative thoughts about what you want, you let doubt lead you and start small. When the universe starts answering your (small) affirmations, you let bad feelings take the lead; you start to feel as if you deserve better, and end up not showing appreciation for whatever the universe has gifted to you. Thus you start to vibrate negativity, which in turn attracts negative results into your life, and so the cycle continues.

On the flip side, even those with positive thoughts want to change everything in their life in a moment. Effectively, they become the reincarnation of Icarus, flying too near the sun. What happens is that they experience huge resistance (vibrational resistance) due to the underlying negative thoughts that show their dissatisfaction with their current self. With this kind of mindset, it is very hard to manifest your affirmations. In such a case, it's necessary to reverse the process that makes you attract negative thoughts and use it to attract positive thoughts into your life. Once you do that, you will start transforming your personal vibration through having smaller thoughts that will not have much difficulty in manifesting. The more successful manifestations you experience in your life, the sooner you will start to enter into your desired vibrational zone.

When that happens, you will experience true belief that your affirmations are being fulfilled, thus allowing you to experience even greater manifestations. You could describe this as expanding your vibrational reach, or entering into a new vibrational zone. At this time, your vibrational frequency and the vibrational frequency for the manifestation of what you want in your life will be fairly equal resulting, in less difficulty in manifesting. With continuous practice and expansion of your vibrational reach, you will ultimately attract any and all of your desires with relative ease.

You won't look at the reasons why something didn't happen in your life. You will look for ways to make it happen. That's the difference between the negative and positive energy that people put into their lives. I once went back to visit my hometown and found someone that I had known from childhood who was unhappy then and is still unhappy and unfulfilled now. Why?

They don't expect anything to happen in their life. They don't see themselves as entitled to anything. They fill their life with jealousy for what other people have and that jealousy kills off all positivity and the vibes are so bad that they will never achieve happiness. That's a sad state of affairs and if you know anyone who is like this, then suggesting they learn about the Law of Attraction may actually help them within their lives. In my case, I wasn't able to help the person because they were so deeply entrenched in their negative world that they could not see the wood for the trees.

Nathan Powers

Chapter 4

Master the Art of Creating Powerful Affirmations

Although affirmations may seem like empty words, they have creative power and a specific vibrational frequency that determines whether you will attract that which you want to attract. Although affirmations generally need to be said in certain circumstances, you don't necessarily need to use them in such circumstances for them to be effective. Remember, the more you are in a certain vibrational zone, the more you attract whatever is within that vibrational zone. In this case, when your thoughts constantly revolve around your affirmations or when you say the things that you want to manifest in your life, it becomes easier for whatever you want to happen to manifest instantly.

You will start living the future you want for yourself when you continuously recite your affirmations. Although you can keep these affirmations in a diary, having the right mindset of how to create powerful affirmations for different situations is actually important if you wish to lower the vibrational gap between your current vibrational frequency and the vibrational frequency you need to be in if you are to manifest whatever you want. Here are some tips to follow when creating affirmations for anything in your life:

Your affirmations shouldn't have negatives; always stay positive

Don't include don'ts in your affirmations. For instance, if you don't want to be poor, say 'The universe is full of riches for me to tap' as opposed to 'I don't want to be poor.' Even if you don't want something, having the mindset that you simply don't want it and want something different won't actually give you anything different. You will attract poverty your way if you have don'ts in your affirmations that relate to your finances. Haven't you yet realized that the things you fear most in your life tend to happen most to you?

For instance, if you continuously affirm that you don't want bad dreams, you will probably have bad dreams whether you like it or not. The universe doesn't differentiate between what you want and what you don't want; if something is in your thoughts, you will attract it! Even if you haven't been thinking of poverty in the recent past, you could attract poverty. This can happen if your thinking about poverty is still within close proximity to the vibrational frequency you were in at the time when your thoughts about poverty occupied a major part of your subconscious mind.

Your subconscious mind is like a radio - broadcasting to the universe everything about you, including your fears, wants, perceptions, likes, desires and everything you could imagine. Remember, you cannot fool yourself into believing affirmations when your subconscious mind has some doubts regarding your ability to manifest what you want in your life. Those subconscious doubts are actually the ones that cause vibrational reverberations that come back to haunt you, even if you haven't actually been vibrating the wrong kind of energy recently.

For your wants to be manifested instantly, you must keep away from those recurring thoughts and habits that make you go back to the doubtful self that attracts negative energy, resulting in manifestations of undesirable outcomes in your life.

Keep Your Affirmations Affirmative

Affirming alone isn't enough; you need to keep your affirmations strong and motivational if you are to believe them and start living the kind of life you want to live. For instance, your affirmations shouldn't just make you want a manifestation; you should say it as if you have already received your manifestation, so make it strong enough. The more your subconscious mind believes in it, the easier it will be for you to enter into the vibrational zone of your desired life. In short, you are trying to make yourself believe that what you want has already been manifested. With that, you start living in the vibrational zone of whatever you want manifested in your life, which results in a reduced difficulty in manifestation. In real terms, the more you perceive that something has taken place in your life, the more you will actually find it easier to attract it; like attracts like every time.

Keep Your Affirmations Within Your Vibrational Reach

You don't want to set yourself up for frustration or negativity, resulting in a cycle of doubt and disappointment. If you want any of your affirmations to be manifested instantly, ensure they are within or in close proximity to your vibrational reach to ensure that you don't experience difficulty in manifesting. Your level of belief will be determined by how much the degree of difficulty you envisage in order for your manifestations to take place. If you have arrived at the point of believing in infinite possibilities - and be honest with yourself about this - you can then start making wild affirmations that are way outside your vibrational zone and still expect them to manifest with ease.

How To Get Instant Manifestations For All Your Affirmations

Coming up with powerful affirmations is not nearly enough to bring you the needed manifestations instantly. You need to be properly aligned with the things you want to attract if you are to minimize the difficulty in manifesting anything in your life. Actually, this will make you experience instant manifestations of anything you want to happen in your life. So how do you get to the point of preparing yourself to attract whatever you want to manifest in your life?

Change/Master Your Thought Patterns

Thoughts are the creative force that determines what people attract to themselves. Because of this, it is important to prepare yourself to reach the point of controlling what you think so that you can start believing with 100% honesty that what you affirm will manifest in your life. For instance, if you want to be cured of a disease, don't think like a sick person; you should start behaving and thinking like someone who is already cured of his or her disease. This will in turn attract vibrations that you would experience if you were healthy, resulting in instant manifestation with regard to your health. The more you can master your thought balance, the more you can reach a point of attaining an ideal vibrational balance that will continuously allow you to manifest everything you want in your life with ease.

Be Specific On What You Want

You vibrations will definitely attract something, whether desirable or undesirable. Don't just expect the universe to give you anything; have something in mind that you want manifested in your life. If you want a pay hike, affirm how much money you want to be paid. Likewise, if you want to win a lottery, be specific and state how much money you want to win on the lottery. This is the only way you can start vibrating within the vibrational frequency of whatever manifestations you want in your life.

Don't Give Rules To The Universe

In as much as you should be specific about what you want manifested in your life instantly, don't try to be too choosy and specific about how you want your affirmations to be manifested. You should believe that the universe is listening to whatever you usually affirm in your life. The more you concentrate on the how part, the more you will feel as if you don't have what it takes to attract that which you want. Let your infinite vibrations take charge once you have affirmed what you want, and leave the rest to the universe to control. Actually, what you should do next is simply wait for your manifestation to be fulfilled.

Now that you have the basics of the Law of Attraction, and a list of 100 powerful affirmations to use for all sorts of situations, it's time to look more closely and in more detail at how you can make the Law of Attraction work to your advantage, and help you to realize the positive manifestations you want in your life. Look at all areas of your life and recognize those that create negative vibrations because these are the vibrations you need to avoid. You need to walk forward looking at life from a different perspective because in all circumstances, no matter how dire they may appear to be, there are positive aspects and your job is to find them in order to invoke the Law of Attraction and everything that comes with it. It's really completely up to you to do and everyone has the same possibility. Don't ever think that others were born with more chance of happiness and fulfillment than you were. Do you think that actually being rich means that you are fulfilled? It's not about what you own. It's not about what you possess. It's about what you feel inside and what you attract to your life. That's really what everyone needs to understand. Get rid of negative thoughts and learn to use positive vibes to get exactly what you feel you need in life and it will happen.

Nathan Powers

Chapter 5

How Affirmations Actually Work

Everyone thinks all the time, even when they don't think they are thinking! According to research, every person has between 45,000 and 51,000 thoughts each and every day of their lives. That equates to around 150 to 200 thoughts a minute, most of which probably flit through your mind without your even realizing. Here's the killer though – something like 80% of those thoughts – conscious or unconscious – are negative thoughts.

That's not the end of the bad news on thoughts though. Around 90% of today's thoughts will flit through your mind again tomorrow, so that means today's negative thoughts will still be around tomorrow, and you're trapped in a vicious cycle of negativity that prevents you from getting what you really want from life. However, there is a way to change this, and that way is to harness the power of affirmations to train yourself to be more aware of your thoughts and what they really mean to you, both conscious and unconscious. So what exactly is an affirmation?

First of all, let's clear the decks and say what an affirmation is NOT, before talking about what it is. An affirmation is not delusional, unrealistic or a fantasy of the mind. Put simply, an affirmation states that something is so, even when there is dispute about the facts of the matter. It's a short, repeated statement that will help to reprogram your subconscious. An affirmation does not have to be a long phrase, or even a complete sentence, because the subconscious is not concerned about grammar. It does like short stuff though, so the shorter your affirmation the better, although you do need to ensure it clearly states what you want to manifest into your life.

Affirmations create empowering messages in your mind if they are repeated often enough, because the subconscious tends to believe the stuff you repeat consistently, whether it is actually true or not. Once the subconscious mind has grasped what you are affirming, your thought patterns, habits and behavior will subtly change to reflect your new positivity of thought.

Affirmations are motivational, and help you to reach your goals, and they can change your thinking and behavior to attract different people into your circle who can help you achieve your goals in life. To arrive where you really want to be in life, you must have faith, self-belief and confidence, and affirmations can help with that, provided you approach them in the right way. If you don't believe in your affirmations, you can't expect the Powers in the Universe to believe in them either, so you really do have to achieve a major shift in your thought patterns.

It's not enough to just say your affirmation once or twice and then forget about it – they have to be repeated on a daily basis, so that they become drilled into your subconscious. How you achieve this is down to personal preference, but you need some time to yourself, when there are no distractions or interruptions, so that you can focus your mind on your affirmations.

Affirmations should be done daily, then, and you need to set aside a time for them. Say them out loud or say them in your head, but make a conscious effort to articulate them, and visualize them coming to pass. For example, if you want to lose weight, visualize yourself wearing a dress that is a size or two smaller than what you're wearing now. Stand tall, feel good, absorb the admiring glances as you affirm, 'I am fit, I am slim, I am beautiful,' or something along those lines.

Repeat, repeat, repeat, until your subconscious gets the message, then do it all again another day. Depending on the affirmation, it can take weeks or months rather than days until it manifests. However, during that time, you will notice subtle but important changes in your attitude and circumstances – just as long as you hold on to the belief that you will succeed in what you set out to do.

Affirmations need to be 100% positive. So, for example, you will not say 'I don't want to be fat,' you will say 'I am thin and healthy.' Not wanting to be fat is a great goal, but it still smacks of the negative, as does an affirmation like 'I am no longer fat.' This is because your thoughts are still attuned to that negative time when you were fat, and that can be enough to get in the way of your determination to be slim, fit and healthy. By thinking about the time when you were fat, even in a way that says you are pleased that that is no longer the case, you are still focusing on that negative time. That means your thoughts are not entirely positive.

In effect, by still thinking of the bad old days, you are ill wishing your future. In some cultures, people will not articulate negative thoughts, since they believe it makes bad things happen. They will therefore avoid mentioning anything negative in conjunction with themselves or their loved ones.

There is no magic in affirmations, but they do work. And the way they work is through the power of thought, and also the power of action. When you repeat the affirmation that 'I am beautiful,' you will stand tall, ready to be noticed, ready to accept the compliments that you know will come your way, because you are confident in your beauty. That confidence will radiate to those around you, making you more attractive to them. Your thoughts and your actions have made you beautiful. You have affirmed your beauty for all to see. It's not enough to just say it though – you have to BE it. Make sure that you are whatever you affirm, every single time. Have you ever seen someone dress themselves up to look good and then actually make a mess of it by tripping over their high heels? The reason this happens is that they were not aware of their power to attract others just by being themselves. You don't have to wear the right shoes to attract the right attention. The right person with positive vibrations could turn everyone's head even if she was wearing no shoes. That must prove something to you. It's not about what you look like. It's about who you are inside and how much positivity you ooze from every action you take in life.

Nathan Powers

Chapter 6

Using the Law of Attraction to Attract a Partner

The Law of Attraction can be used in all life situations, and one of those which is particularly popular is attracting a lover, partner, and soul mate - whatever you want to call that special someone. All the world loves a lover, and sometimes it can seem like the only person in the world who isn't part of a couple is you. So naturally, you want to find a partner, and you're going to use a powerful affirmation to help you to do so.

But hey – not so fast. Are you really ready for a new relationship? The thing is, before you can be happy as part of a couple, you need to be perfectly happy on your own. If that sounds like a bit of a contradiction, it's not really. It's quite simple – if you are desperate for a partner, then your reasons are almost certainly negative. Maybe you're lonely, or you miss having a man (or woman) around the place. Or perhaps you think you are just not cut out to be alone.

None of these are positive reasons for finding a new life partner. Because under the Law of Attraction like attracts like, these negative reasons will somehow manifest in the partner or within the relationship. It might start off well, and you might even get married and have a family, but there will come a time when the negativity of the original attraction will show itself in one way or another. It may or may not lead to a breakdown of the relationship, but it's sure to result in unhappiness for one or both partners.

The truth of the matter is nobody needs anybody else to be a complete person, but when two positive people come together, they create something special that is much more than the sum of their parts. People who are complete and self-contained are not looking to trade in a relationship, whereas often that is what happens when two people get together. He might be looking for regular sex and someone to cook his meals, while she's after financial security and someone to give her babies. They might not even realize this at the time, but it's there, deep in the subconscious, and while this might seem reasonable to most people, under the Law of Attraction it's just plain wrong.

Trading might work in business and politics, but it doesn't work in relationships, and what you end up with is a dysfunctional union based on fear. He's always striving to earn enough money to keep her and the kids in the style they've become accustomed to, while she worries that the time will come when he'll no longer find her attractive. That's because most people's default position is to plan for catastrophe, to think of the 'What Ifs?' They might think it's responsible behavior, but really, when they dwell on the things that might go wrong in their relationships, they attract the very things they dread.

Enjoy Being You – Right Now!

So how do you get to a stage where you are self-contained and contented, and in perfect shape to attract your ideal partner? First of all, it may sound trite, but you have to love yourself. If you don't, how do you expect anyone else to love you? Loving yourself starts with taking care of yourself. Eat healthily; stay in shape; and keep yourself clean and well groomed; dress with care. In short, be the kind of person you would be attracted to yourself.

Sounds simple when its written on paper, doesn't it? Well, in a way it is, and in a way it isn't. To be that positive person, you have to reprogram your subconscious, so that all your thoughts are positive ones. Then you will experience positive vibrations and attract the positive energy and manifestations that everyone needs in their life, even if they don't always recognize it or even admit it. Write down a list of the things you love about yourself and check it out every day. That way, you will be the person you love.

Don't think about how much better life will be when you have a partner – think about how good life is now, and it will be good. When you radiate self-love, you attract love from others, because people are attracted to positive people who radiate happiness, but they are repelled by negative people. If you don't love yourself, you can't expect others to love you.

Be Positive About What You Want from a Partner

The whole point about the Law of Attraction is that like always attracts like, and that needs to be repeated until it's engraved on your soul. So when you're writing affirmations to attract a partner, you have to couch them in positive terms. It might sound reasonable to say that you don't want a guy who puts work or friends before his significant other, but that is a negative expression, which is likely to bring exactly what you don't want into your relationship. Instead say something like 'I am lucky to be with a man who works hard and always finds time to support his friends.'

Doesn't that sound so much more positive? Notice that the affirmation is in the present tense, and there's an 'I' in it, to identify the affirmation with yourself. It's your life that you want to attract this ideal partner into, so you need to put yourself in the forefront. And once you do meet that special person, keep it positive by not allowing negative emotions such as jealousy and neediness to come between you.

Keep the Faith

Believe that your affirmations will manifest, and don't allow doubts to creep in. Remember like attracts like, and if you don't believe you will ever find a mate, then you won't. Don't give up on it – anything that's worth having is worth waiting for. People seem to think that all their desires will instantly manifest, and indeed some do, but others take a little longer, and everything that happens to you happens for a reason. Those dates that you wish you had never turned up for had a purpose, because they helped to remind you what you don't want in a partner, thereby making it all the more special when the right person comes along. And if you can learn to see these so-called failed dates in a more positive light, you will attract a more suitable partner.

Part of the cycle of doubt and disbelief is wondering how things will happen. Don't even go there- just believe that you will find the love of your life, or the perfect partner for you. Happiness in love is on its way to you, and you only need to know and believe that it is – you really don't need to be involved in the how. In any case, that's outside human understanding. Just prepare yourself for love and it will manifest in your life.

Prepare for Love and Enjoy the Now

You don't need to wait for love to have fun, because you don't need love in order to enjoy yourself. You don't need anything or anybody, because you contain everything you really need for happiness. A loving partner is just the icing on the cake, and if you get out and enjoy yourself, rather than waiting home alone for Mr. or Miss Right, your special someone will find you, because you will stand out from the crowd.

Think how your life will be when you meet your match, and be that person now – don't wait for him or her to make you that person, because you can do it all yourself, and you can do it now. If you think you will be more confident and loving when you have a partner, you can be confident and loving now – you don't need validation from anyone else.

On a more practical level, prepare your living space for your partner. You've already made room for him or her in your heart; now make room in your home. Clear some space they can call their own when they are with you. Spend the waiting time preparing for love, so that when it manifests, you are ready to enjoy perfect alignment with the partner you have always dreamed of.

Nathan Powers

Chapter 7

Using the Law of Attraction to Attract Wealth

You can attract wealth by utilizing the Law of Attraction, and just as in looking for love, your thoughts and vibrations need to be positive if you are to achieve the wealth you want in your life. When it comes to money, you can prepare the way to remove your negative thoughts by consciously becoming more proactive in managing your finances. Think of money as your friend, and visualize yourself with all the money you need. Imagine having that money in your hands, and imagine what it feels like to have all the money you want. In the meantime, you can take steps to move yourself towards that state.

The most important thing you can do is to arrange to pay your bills on time, so that you are not worrying about debts. This creates negative vibrations, because when there are obligations people cannot meet, whether financial, professional or personal, they become fearful. Not only that, you cannot truly focus your thoughts on making money if you owe money. The negative cancels out the positive here.

Alongside this, list all your expenditures so you can identify areas where savings can be made, and create a realistic, workable budget. If all this seems like a lot of hard work, think of it as removing the negative money-related aspects from your life. You are preparing the way for abundance by being proactive in reducing debt and managing your money wisely. Remember to be thankful for what you have, rather than wishing for what you do not have, because those are negative thoughts, and they will return negative manifestations. Now you are ready to harness the Law of Attraction to attract wealth and abundance to you and your loved ones.

The first thing to realize is that wealth does not relate exclusively to money, and you can be wealthy in your life even if you do not have a lot of money. This is where being thankful comes in. If you are desperate for money – for example, if you focus your thoughts on winning the lottery to solve all your financial problems – then you will actually repel money and attract more desperation. It's all those negative thoughts surfacing again.

One thing you need to remember is that you get exactly what you ask for. So, if you ask to be a millionaire, but don't ask for the things you might want to buy with that million dollars, you won't get them. What you ask for, you will get, so be specific in your requests. Here are some ideas to help you maximize the potential for attracting money.

Shift Your Focus Regarding Bills And Debts

It's a natural response to complain when the bills come in, and of course, those are negative responses. 'How did we run up such a big bill on the credit card?' is not useful. Telling yourself that you are grateful that you used the credit card to pay for a new washing machine so that you can keep the family's clothes clean with ease demonstrates gratitude. Gratitude for a credit card bill might sound a bit surreal, but that's the way you're going to have to program your subconscious if you want to use the Law of Attraction to attract money.

Think of the things you have been able to do as a result of using electricity, for example. You've cooked food for the family, been entertained by the television, and had light during the hours of darkness so you could read, work on the computer or catch up with friends through Facebook. Put like that, it's almost a privilege to have that electric bill to pay, isn't it?

Realize How Much Abundance Is Already In Your Life

Okay, maybe you are not a millionaire – yet – but you are rich in other ways. You have a roof over your head, food to eat, and an abundance of friends who care for you. Just get into that mindset that everything is something to be grateful for, and that you have an abundance of good, useful and beautiful things in your life, and you will soon attract more abundance, because, as you know, like attracts like. And the type of abundance you will attract will be what you really want, what you have asked for, whether that is money, possessions or even both. If you consider yourself to be rich in non-financial ways, then eventually you will be rich in money and possessions. It's all about reprogramming your subconscious to open your mind to the reception of wealth and abundance. If you think negative thoughts then it will attract negativity. So don't think you don't have enough or that you could have been a billionaire if it weren't for your fate. You have a lot now and you have to feel blessed for having all of it. If you think what you have now is a lot then wealth and money will keep coming into your life.

Love Money

The old saying that 'Money is the root of all evil' is not true. Money itself is not evil – it is a thing, not a person, it does not have characteristics or a conscience. It is the way some people use money that is evil, not money itself. So there is no reason not to love money – it can do a lot of good, and if you have money, you can do a lot of good with it too, for yourself, your family, and those you love.

Spend money – enjoy spending it, and enjoy using the goods and services you can buy with it. Build an affinity with money – love the smell of it and the touch of it. Love what it can do to improve your life. You have to literally fall in love with it.

To attract money into your life, you have to think of it in a positive way, so that you can radiate positive vibrations and attract that which you are thinking about. Let go of your negative thoughts about money, bills and debt and celebrate its existence. On the other hand, don't be greedy or miserly. These are negative emotions that will repel the wealth you are seeking.

Above all, don't envy the success of others – it's a fruitless emotion and it will not result in success coming your way. If you criticize or envy their success, it will not help you to draw success to yourself. In fact, envy is a real barrier to receiving abundance.

Nathan Powers

Chapter 8

Using the Law of Attraction for Professional Success

It is possible to have the career of your dreams. There's nothing better than getting paid for doing what you would gladly do free of charge, but how exactly do you harness the Law of Attraction to help you in your career? For a start, once you turn your thoughts to the positive, and become motivated and energized, you attract like-minded people, along with their contacts, who may be very useful to you in your career. In addition, you will attract projects that are designed to bring out the best in you professionally.

How does this happen? It's largely a matter of confidence. In all walks of life, people who succeed do so because they expect nothing less. And if things don't work out in the first place, they will find a work around to ensure that things work better next time around. They don't recognize failure – as Thomas Edison famously said: 'I have not failed – I just found 10,000 ways that did not work.' Failure, or more properly the sense of failure, is another negative emotion, and negativity will block the positive vibrations and prevent your wishes from manifesting.

If you're unemployed and looking for a job, you can harness the Law of Attraction to help you in your job search, but before it can help you need to feel positive about being unemployed. Learn to view this time as a valuable and unexpected opportunity to spend more time with your friends and family, or to devote extra time to a favorite hobby. Never, ever feel negative about your lack of employment, and banish any thoughts that you might never get a job, or that certain jobs are not worth applying for.

Infuse yourself with confidence, walk tall and believe that you will get that job. If you can do that, you can and will snag the job you want, because you will perform well at the interview. Even if you don't get the job – be positive about it. Clearly this job is not the best fit for you, and something better is around the corner.

While you're waiting for your new job to materialize, you can prepare for the success you know is around the corner. Sort out a new work wardrobe – maybe you could use a new briefcase. Check on the prices of season tickets for the boat or train, or have the car serviced so it won't let you down on the way to work. You can also do a number of things to help your job search in a proactive way.

List What You Want From Your Job

Affirmations and positive thoughts are always better and more effective when written down, because it makes them easier to visualize and focus on. Make a list of all the things you want from your job, and couch them in positive terms. For example, don't say 'I don't want to work weekends,' say 'I want to work Monday to Friday so that I can spend the weekends with my friends and family.' Write about the type of boss you would like to work for, how many colleagues would make a perfect working environment, what length of commute you envisage – basically, as many details about your job as you can think of. And remember – everything should be positive if your affirmations are to work and manifest into the job of your dreams.

Know That There Are Enough Jobs To Go Around

There are enough jobs for everyone who wants them, despite what the doom and gloom merchants try to tell you, and that means there is a job just waiting for you. There is plenty of work to go around, and if someone else gets the job you wanted, that means it wasn't meant for you in the first place. Something better I waiting for you, so keep the faith, and don't lose heart. If you allow it to get to you then you will never progress. Remember that positivity is essential and you have to be as positive as possible in order to progress.

You can use the strategies outlined above to work for a promotion or a raise. This is where visualization really comes into its own, because you need to see yourself in the new position. Imagine how you will feel when you are invited to apply for promotion, or when the boss offers you a raise in recognition of your achievements. Visualize your colleagues congratulating you, and think of the things you can do with the extra money. Promotion often means more paid holiday time off work, so maybe your visualization will include a fantastic family vacation to somewhere you've always wanted to go but could never afford.

Live the promotion as if it's already happened. Be in the present tense, reaping the benefits of your new position. Be happy in your work, and love the new freedoms of being higher up the career ladder. Write some new affirmations, and repeat them often. Believe in the power of your affirmations and keep the faith, even when things don't seem to be going your way. Make that especially when things don't seem to be going your way! You can achieve promotion, and you will achieve promotion with the help of the Law of Attraction.

Chapter 9

Using the Law of Attraction for Weight Loss

Most women – and a lot of men – have faced a battle with the bulge at some time in their life. Losing weight is a positive thing to do – especially if carrying excess weight is affecting your health and self-esteem – and the Law of Attraction can help you to do this. However, in this area – possibly more than any other area of your life – you really need to get a grip on your thoughts, and harness positive energy to help you achieve your goal.

People who are overweight or obese often hate their bodies, but if you are going to harness the Law of Attraction to help you lose weight, you need to convert that hate to love. This is where problems can arise, because overweight people think they will feel much better about themselves once they lose weight. However, if you are using the Law of Attraction to help you lose weight, you need to love yourself and be happy before that can happen.

Your previous weight loss efforts have probably including continual thinking about calories, different diets, exercise, and the foods you mustn't eat – all the negative stuff that is anathema to positive affirmation. Now you need to imagine yourself slim and fit, walking into a room and heads turning because you look so darn hot. Imagine how happy you will be, and be happy now, because what you wish is going to happen if you believe in it strongly enough. Act like you're already there, because that shows that you believe you can lose weight, and it will accelerate the energy shift needed to make it happen.

The Gratitude Trick

One way to help you toward the body you want is to express gratitude every day, as if that body is already yours. If you want a slimmer waist, stand in front of the mirror and say 'Thank you for my lovely slim waist.' Like attracts like, so in no time, you will achieve that slim waist you desire, because things will enter your life to make it possible. Maybe you'll hear of a new exercise that's guaranteed to slim your waist, or your friend will tell you how since she's been going to Zumba classes, she's lost 4" from her waist. That's your signal to high tail down to the next class and work on your own waist. See how it works?

You need to be specific about this – don't just say 'I want to be thin,' say where you want to be thin, and then express gratitude as if it has already happened. Before too long, it will happen, as long as you focus on what you want and don't listen to people who try to tell you that your body is just fine as it is. If you're not happy with it, then it's clearly not fine, and you don't need that kind of negativity from people who should be supporting your efforts.

You need to remind yourself that you are in total control of your body – what you put into it, what you put on it, and how and when you move it around. It therefore follows that you have the power to change your body if you are not completely happy with it. However, you can only change your body from an unhealthy one to a healthy one of your mind is also healthy. Most of the work you do on weight loss will take part in your mind, because even those who lose weight by more conventional methods admit that until they are in the right frame of mind, they do not succeed in losing weight. How much more important is it then when you are using a system that depends on harnessing positive thought processes and energy to bring about change?

Body image is a big thing where weight loss is concerned, and that can present a problem, because people who need to lose weight almost always have a negative body image. The trick here is to find a part of your body you love, and wouldn't want to change, and focus your thoughts on that. For example, you may have beautiful, 'come to bed' eyes. For now, focus on those eyes, and be grateful for them every day. Whenever you think of another body part that isn't so bad, or downright lovely, include that too.

Like attracts like, and soon you'll be finding more really nice areas of your body. As the numbers build, you'll come to realize that you do have a body to love and then the positive energy you attract will help make even more improvements to your body.

When you use the Law of Attraction to help with weight loss, you are actually performing a very useful function, because if you have been overweight for a long time, you need to change your thought patterns as well as your eating patterns, because what you eat is only a small part of your weight problem. What also needs to be considered is the part your mind plays in all this. Positive affirmation helps to turn your thoughts around and create positive energy so that you are happy with your body and with your life. When you reach this stage, your weight loss campaign is assured of success.

Chapter 10

Using the Law of Attraction for Health and Wellness

The Law of Attraction is about like attracting like. If your thoughts are negative, you will attract negative energy and people into your circle. And it gets worse when it comes to your health and wellbeing, because people who continually think negative thoughts may see those thoughts manifested as illness in the body. This is because stress and anxiety can compromise the immune system, meaning that the body is more susceptible to physical illness, and les able to fight off threats to the body's wellbeing.

One of the most important things you can do to be healthy is to de-stress your life to allow you more time for relaxation – more 'Me Time.' They say that laughter is the best medicine, and it certainly is a stress buster, as it releases 'feel good' hormones and enzymes to counteract the stress hormones that are released when the body is under physical or mental pressure. So watch and listen to things that make you laugh, and hang around with lively, funny friends. It all helps to keep the stress at bay.

If you are sick, you may think that you'd like to harness the Law of Attraction for healing. However, this would be a mistake, because although healing is a positive thing, it's also a reflection back on the bad health problems you have been experiencing. Rather than focusing on healing, fix your attention and energy on good health and wellness. It's all about states. Healing is a process to shift the state of the body from a negative state (sickness) to a positive one (wellness). Wellness is everyone's desired state of being, so it is a happy and desirable state to be in.

Change Your Perspective On Illness

Another positive way to view illness is to look at it from a different aspect. For example, if you have arthritis, and you can no longer walk comfortably, you can still swim, since the water will support your joints. And swimming can be very enjoyable, so instead of being sad that you can't go for long walks any more, be thankful that you can enjoy a swim any time you want. Focus on what you have, rather than what your condition has taken away from you. This will help you to get into the positive frame of mind you need if the Law of Attraction is going to help you to achieve good health.

It's a useful exercise to write down the limitations your health condition places on you. Then, on the other side of the paper, write down the things you can still do, and the things you have gained through your illness. For instance, maybe you can no longer work, or you may have to work reduced hours because of your condition. That frees up time to pursue hobbies, take a course or join a club, or just spend some time reading or relaxing. There are benefits in every state of being – it's just that sometimes you have to look a little harder to find them.

Another exercise in perspective changing is to stop and think what's working okay within your body. Maybe you have a problem with your lungs, but your brain is functioning normally, so are your liver and kidneys. And your hearing and eyesight is perfect. Focus attention away from the body parts that are not working, as they should, and towards the perfect bits. Give thanks for their perfect working order, and see that gratitude returned, because you get back what you put in with the Law of Attraction. As you concentrate on your lists, you may even find that you are not in so much discomfort, because your brain has something else to focus on. That's another plus of positive energy generation.

As with all cases where the Law of Attraction is harnessed to bring improvement, your affirmations must be positive, in the present tense and specific to you, as if you are already living life in good health. Another important point is to focus fully on the end result, but don't waste your thoughts on how that result will be achieved. That's not part of your remit. Your mission – should you choose to accept it – is to reprogram your consciousness so that the majority of your thoughts are positive. That's because like attracts like, and positive thoughts will bring positive energy to you in order to help you to achieve or maintain wellness. You do not need to know how that will be achieved, or when. You just need to believe with all your heart that it will happen. That's all that is required of you – you can safely leave the logistics to the greater Powers in the Universe.

Conclusion

The Law of Attraction can be reduced to a short, simple sentence at its most basic level: 'Like attracts like.' However, there is a great deal more to it than that. Harnessing the power of the Law of Attraction requires a firm commitment to improving your life and reprogramming your subconscious so that it radiates positive energy. Of the 45,000 – 51,000 thoughts almost every person has every day, around 80% of those are negative thoughts. Staying with the numbers, 90% of each day's thoughts will move on to the next day, so the negative vibes are augmented.

It therefore takes time, effort and commitment to turn those thoughts around so that positive vibrations are sent out into the universe. The upside of positive thoughts and behaviors is that they attract positive things and people to them, just as negative thoughts and behaviors can attract angry people and illness. It's a challenging task, but it can be done, and the more you practice positive affirmation, the easier it becomes.

Affirmations are short, repeated statements of intention which must be couched in positive terms, in the present tense and with a specific 'I am' statement or something similar to align the affirmation with you and also identify it as yours. The present tense is used because it is important to visualize yourself in the desired state. You should act as if you are already slim and fit, healthy or rich, because putting out that positive energy and aligning yourself with the states you want to enjoy is a great way to manifest your desires.

You can use ready written affirmations, or you can write your own, but they need to be short and succinct rather than long and rambling, since they have to be repeated, and you need to focus your mind on them as you work with them. It is probably better to write your own, because they come straight from the heart, and they are deeply personal, so they are more likely to work for you. Also, you will probably be more comfortable with something that you have written yourself and believe in wholeheartedly.

The Law of Attraction can be used to bring success, fulfillment and contentment in all areas of life, and it is most commonly used in love and relationships, career development, wealth and money management, health and wellbeing and weight loss. Its powers can also be helpful to people fighting addictions such as drugs, nicotine and alcohol, since the positive energy is an excellent counterbalance for the negativity of addiction.

The positive mindset does not mean that people coast through life without problems, but because they have a positive outlook on life, they are better equipped to find solutions to those problems. It's a similar scenario with success – they expect success, but if it doesn't always happen, they find a work around because their minds are not bogged down with negative, defeatist thoughts. They believe themselves, and are able to solve problems because they are confident and have no doubts or fears.

Positive thinkers do not rely on others for happiness or completion – they are happy now, and friends and lovers are pleasant additions to their worlds, not essentials for happiness and fulfillment. These people are self-confident and self-contained, and because they radiate confidence, they are more attractive to others.

In the same way, negative thinkers repel happy, balanced people and attract like-minded individuals, so they are never truly happy or contented. People are not born positive or negative – it's learned behavior, borne of upbringing, experiences and influences. Therefore it is possible to reprogram the consciousness using positive affirmations and the power of positive thought to find advantages in even the bleakest scenarios. It's 'Every cloud has a silver lining' but more far-reaching.

If the Law of Attraction is to work for you, you need to consciously clear your mind of all negative thoughts. You also need to be specific in what you want, what you expect from your affirmations. However, you should not waste energy on wondering how your wishes will be met. That is not part of your remit, and you will not gain from knowing, even if it were possible. Debating the 'how' demonstrates a lack of trust and faith, and that pretty much guarantees that the Law of Attraction will not work for you.

You're going to need patience and persistence too, because you will have to repeat your affirmations several times a day, for weeks or maybe months. And through all that, you have to keep the faith. This is not for the faint hearted! Doubts and disbelief have no place in the Law of Attraction. Believe that it works, because it does, whether you know it or not.

There are spiritual and scientific explanations for why the Law of Attraction works. Spiritually, there is a belief that God and the universe align with our wishes when the frequency of energy is changed by positive thinking. The science bit believes that people who are more open minded naturally take more risks and thus notice opportunities more and are eager for new experiences. Therefore things find them rather than them having to go looking.

There's more to it than positive thinking though – action is also required. You have to give yourself the best opportunity for success by doing things that will make your life how you want it. For example, if you are using the Law of Attraction to attract wealth, you need to be proactive in managing your finances as they stand by paying off debts, creating a budget and curtailing unnecessary expenditure. Likewise, if you're looking for love, you have to be the kind of person that attracts love, so you need to be happy and considerate, and you also need to get out and socialize so you have the opportunities to meet new people.

Some people say the Law of Attraction doesn't work, and usually that's because they don't really understand the guiding principles. They expect a quick fix – which it's not – and they don't put enough effort into banishing negativity from their thoughts. There is a great deal of anecdotal and empirical evidence to show that the Law of Attraction does work, in all sorts of circumstances, for all sorts of people.

If you have stayed with the book this far, you're probably wondering if the Law of Attraction can work for you. The answer is: yes it can, but you also have to work with it to achieve the results you want and get the life you dream of living. Concentrate on positive thoughts, positive affirmations and visualizations of your dreams and desires.

Help yourself to happiness by looking after your mind and body. Eat healthy, exercise, and try to keep stress in your life to a minimum. Be happy in the now - don't wait for a new job, a new guy or girl, or a new figure to bring happiness, because that is not going to happen. You are in sole charge of your body and your life, and while you cannot control everything that happens, you can control your reactions to the events and people that affect you in major or minor ways. Always take the positives from situations, and discount the negatives. Take 'I wish' and 'If only' out of your vocabulary and look for the benefits and bonuses in every situation.

This all sounds like a tall order, but once you get into the positive mindset, it will all start to come naturally. The Law of Attraction and positive affirmations can make a real difference in your life if you are open to its infinite possibilities. Go ahead and check it out – test the power of positive thinking. You have nothing to lose, and everything in the universe to gain.

Publisher's Note

Leave a review, get a free book!

Dear Customer,

If you have time, we'd love it if you would write a short, honest review of this book. Your feedback helps us improve our books as we work very closely with our authors to provide you with quality material. Since we are small publishing company, we rely on customers like you to share their experiences with our books with other customers on Amazon. Keeping our marketing costs low helps us keep our books reasonably priced. We truly appreciate every review we get, and your comments. Reviews can be done quickly here:

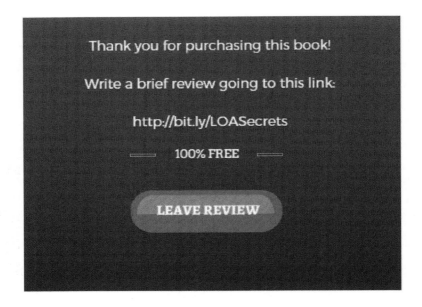

Just send us the link to your review at catalystpublishers@gmail.com and we'll get you LEADERSHIP 100% FREE!

NOTE: If there were any issues with this book, please contact us so we resolve them.

Don't forget to sign up for our Free Book Promotion emails as well!

Your Free Instant Manifestation Gift!

As a way of saying "thank you" for downloading this book, I'd like to offer you even more access to powerful tools that have helped me change my entire life and manifest the success, relationships and financial freedom that I want YOU to enjoy!

Get *"The secret to manifestation: 10 proven every day rituals to effectively apply the law of attraction"* totally FREE!

I used to think all of these things would never come to me because it was "hard" and I wasn't raised by financially well off parents – not by a long shot. The Law of Attraction has changed my entire life and I'm so excited to share these powerful tools with you, that I'm giving them to you TOTALLY FREE just go to the link!

Write this link on your browser: http://bit.ly/SecretManifestation

Thanks,

Nathan Powers

Check out my other books

Check out my other titles on Amazon and Kindle:

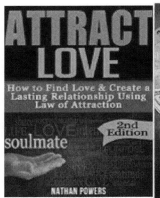
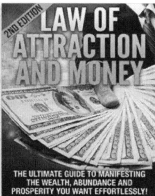

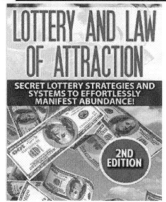

The Law of Attraction and Money – The Ultimate Guide to Manifesting The Wealth, Abundance and Prosperity You Want Effortlessly! http://bit.ly/LOAMoney

The Law of Attraction and Weight Loss – Practical Steps to Change Your Mindset, Lose Weight and Finally Manifest Your Dream Body http://bit.ly/LOAWeightLoss

The Law of Attraction and the Lottery – Secret Lottery Strategies and Systems to Effortlessly Manifest Abundance! http://bit.ly/LOALottery

Attract Love: How to Find Love & Create A Lasting Relationship Using Law of Attraction – 2nd Edition http://bit.ly/LOALove

Sneak Preview of "The Lottery and Law of Attraction

Secret Lottery Strategies and Systems to Effortlessly Manifest Abundance"

The Law of Attraction

The law of attraction is one of the 12 laws of the universe, it states that you attract what you will, and positive vibrations lead to positive results while negative vibrations lead to negative results. The easiest method by which to understand this principal is to look at an example of a scenario where it may apply. A young boy was watching another boy whom they went to school with, ride his new bicycle. He was overcome by a feeling of want, and decided that he must have a bicycle for himself. He went home that evening with a smile on his face sure that he would soon get a bicycle to call his. He took a baseball and bat and waited on the porch for his father to come home from work. While he was seated there, looking out onto the street, he could see himself riding the bicycle around the block and competing with his friend, who had a bicycle. With a smile on his face and the belief that he would get a bicycle soon, he patiently waited for his father for more than five hours, not for a moment did he doubt, or think, what if I don't get it? He was so sure that he would get his heart's desire.

Now, you might ask yourself, how could he be so sure that he would get it? Perhaps it was that he had a lot of faith in his father, or that he knew his dad would move heaven and earth to grant him his heart's desire. Regardless, he believed that he would soon have a brand new bike. As the father got out of his car, the boy ran to him, threw his arms around him, and told him to play catch with him. The father overcome by emotions of love for the boy simply put his work briefcase on the porch stairs, took off his work jacket, and went to throw the ball around with son. After throwing the ball a couple of times, he told his father that he wished to have a bicycle for his birthday that was a couple of weeks away. The father told him that he would look into it and see if their finances would let him buy the bicycle.

He looked as his son's faced turned from one of happiness to that of fear; the fear of not getting a bike. He promised himself that he would get his son a bicycle. The boy knew that his father would come through for him. He had so much faith in this that, every day he would tell his dad about how much fun they would have together on his new bike. Every time the father would be filled with joy as the thought of teaching his son how to ride a bicycle filled his thoughts. Funny enough, the father also knew he would not fail to give his son the bicycle. As attraction states, you attract what you will; one week later he got a huge bonus and rushed to the cycle mart where he bought a bicycle and sneaked it into the house. On the birthday morning, the boy groggy with sleep came down the stairs in his pajamas and found a bow tied bike at the foot of the stairs. This is how the law of attraction works. As humans, we may believe in what we want to achieve or get but get distracted by negative emotions.

The Law of Attraction and Lottery

Can the law of attraction help you win the lottery? Many experts have said that the law of attraction may not work on this basing their arguments that it may be a selfish want that the universe may not support. There are instances where many people have used this same law effectively and won a lottery. Do you think that winning the lottery is just a chance or miracle? Well, think again. A while back, I was reading a story of a woman from the Unites States, Cynthia Stamford, who won a first division lottery jackpot of $112 million. Many questions have been raised on whether she used the law of attraction to visualize winning, the answer is yes.

While she was being interviewed, she talked of how she constantly visualized the kind of lifestyle she would have if she had that kind of money. She wrote the figure she wanted to win on a piece of paper and constantly visualized and obsessively focused on this amount for four months. Two weeks later, she bought a ticket and won. While you can visualize, you need to understand why it is you want to win the lottery. Suffice to say, spending all your monthly pay on tickets so as to get yourself out of debt is a bit short sighted. It is limiting oneself to just one stream of "income" and if money is your end goal then perhaps you should opt to look for another financial option rather that restrict yourself to just the lottery.

Publisher's Bonus

Subscribe to Get INSTANT ACCESS to Our Books When They are FREE on Amazon and Kindle!

Go to this link to subscribe: http://bit.ly/PublisherBookSqueeze

We're committed to giving you powerful, quality e-books to help you change your life! Our authors cover a range of topics, all designed to help you live your best life.

Subscribe now if you're interested in:

- Law of Attraction
- Financial Freedom
- Creativity
- Leadership
- Weight Loss
- Self Esteem

BONUS: FREE copy of THINK AND GROW RICH by Napoleon Hill!

Printed in Great Britain
by Amazon